PUB WALKS

— IN —

Staffordshire

THIRTY CIRCULAR WALKS
AROUND STAFFORDSHIRE INNS

Nick Channer

COUNTRYSIDE BOOKS
NEWBURY, BERKSHIRE

First Published 1995
© Nick Channer 1995
Revised and updated 2000

All rights reserved. No reproduction
permitted without the prior permission
of the publishers:

COUNTRYSIDE BOOKS
3 Catherine Road
Newbury, Berkshire

To view our complete range of books,
please visit us at
www.countrysidebooks.co.uk

ISBN 1 85306 360 6

Designed by Mon Mohan
Cover illustration by Colin Doggett
Photographs by the author
Maps by Jack Street

Produced through MRM Associates Ltd., Reading
Typeset by The Midlands Book Typesetting Company, Loughborough
Printed and bound by J W Arrowsmith Ltd., Bristol

Contents

Publisher's Note

We hope that you obtain considerable enjoyment from this book; great care has been taken in its preparation. However, changes of landlord and actual closures are sadly not uncommon. Likewise, although at the time of publication all routes followed public rights of way or permitted paths, diversion orders can be made and permissions withdrawn.

We cannot of course be held responsible for such diversion orders and any inaccuracies in the text which result from these or any other changes to the routes nor any damage which might result from walkers trespassing on private property. However we are anxious that all details covering the walks and the pubs are kept up to date and would therefore welcome information from readers which would be relevant to future editions.

Area map showing locations of the walks.

Introduction

Staffordshire, lying at the heart of England, is one of our largest counties. The growth of the Black Country and the Pottery towns made it synonymous for so long with smoking chimneys and the grime of industry, and yet within its boundaries is some of the most spectacular and diverse scenery to be found anywhere in Britain. Staffordshire has never completely lost its old reputation, but these days its image is a good deal cleaner and greener.

Anyone not entirely familiar with Staffordshire will discover many attractions within the county. To the south lies Cannock Chase, an oasis of heather heathland, deep valleys and indigenous woodland, designated an Area of Outstanding Natural Beauty in the 1950s. On occasions you may catch a glimpse of fallow deer moving silently between the softwoods, or red squirrels, now sadly in decline, skipping along the branches of oak and beech trees.

The southernmost tip of Staffordshire protrudes like a finger, pointing down into the huge urban sprawl of the West Midlands. Here, surprisingly, there are delightful, unspoilt pockets of countryside to explore on the Worcestershire border. For example, the sandstone ridge of Kinver Edge is probably one of the most popular beauty spots in this part of the county. The fertile farming country and parkland estates of mid and south Staffordshire offer widespread views and the opportunity to stroll in peaceful surroundings.

However, the northern half of Staffordshire is the most scenically dramatic. East of the Potteries the river Churnet snakes through the 'Staffordshire Rhineland', beneath glorious wooded banks and through spectacular gorges, on its way to meet the Dove. This is *Adam Bede* country. One of Britain's most influential novelists, George Eliot – otherwise Mary Ann Evans – set her first novel in this part of Staffordshire, calling the county Loamshire. North of here the Dove meanders between the emerald green hills of the southern Peak District, where the scenery around the village of Alstonefield, close to the county's north-east boundary, is truly glorious. Further north still are The Roaches, an eerie, primaeval chain of wild gritstone hills forming part of the Staffordshire Moorlands. It is indeed true that at every turn Staffordshire reveals yet another new and unexpected face.

Ingrained in the county's character is its fascinating industrial heritage. There are many reminders of Staffordshire's working past, not least among them is the name of Josiah Wedgwood, 'Father of the Pottery Industry'. The canal system, which criss-crosses the county and today is acknowledged as an important leisure facility, is a permanent tribute to the skill and genius of its engineers. There are a number of inns located on Staffordshire's waterways and some of their memorabilia reflect canal life and the culture of the boat people.

The walks chosen for this book are, on the whole, short and relatively undemanding, providing a few hours' entertainment in the fresh air. The Staffordshire Way runs like a thread through the county and many of the described routes coincide with stretches of it. All the walks are circular, beginning and finishing at a traditional local hostelry where food is available. Many of the inns welcome children, some allow dogs, all of them permit walkers.

There is a general description of the pub, including details of its menu. All of them have a car park where you can leave a vehicle whilst out on the walk. However, several landlords have specifically requested that those wishing to do this should notify the staff beforehand. The opening hours are 'standard', unless otherwise stated, that is 11 am or 11.30 am to 2.30 pm at lunchtimes, 6.30 pm or 7 pm to 11 pm in the evenings (reduced slightly on Sundays). Telephone numbers are given.

As a safeguard, I would urge you to carry a copy of the Ordnance Survey map, as well as basic waterproof clothing and a good pair of walking shoes. Something more robust should be worn in very wet conditions, when the ground can become waterlogged.

Finally, I hope you enjoy the delights of the Staffordshire countryside, its genuine country inns, its many miles of public rights of way, and its splendid scenery.

Nick Channer

1 Kinver
The White Harte

Spectacularly situated amidst hills and woods, the village of Kinver, in the south-west corner of Staffordshire, has long been a favourite haunt of locals and visitors. Its superb position almost gives it the appearance of an alpine community. At the turn of the century a tram company described Kinver as 'the Switzerland of the Midlands'.

The White Harte, located in the centre of the village, is a rambling old coaching inn with an assortment of beams and horse brasses. The building is thought to date back to the early 16th century, and according to local legend there are several secret passages leading to the nearby church. There may also be a connection with the Civil War, or possibly the Battle of Worcester in 1651 – in the course of major structural work to the inn in the 1960s, a Roundhead's helmet was discovered. It is still on show in the bar.

There is a non-smoking conservatory and the inn's menu offers a wide choice of food which is available every day – everything from salmon and cod to gammon and 7oz rump steak. Sandwiches and soup are also available, as are several vegetarian dishes. The evening menu includes spicy Cajun chicken and goujons. There is also a traditional Sunday roast and a specials board. Tempting sweets include chocolate fudge cake and apple pie. Among the beers are Banks's Bitter and Original. There is usually a guest ale. Harp Irish, Guinness and Strongbow and Scrumpy Jack are also available. Children are welcome. Dogs are restricted to the beer garden. Popular barbecues take place in the summer.

Telephone: 01384 872305.

How to get there: Kinver is west of Stourbridge, just off the A449 between Kidderminster and Wolverhampton. The inn is in the High Street.

Parking: The White Harte has its own car park. Alternatively, there is a public car park on the other side of the High Street.

Length of the walk: 3½ miles. Map: OS Landranger 138 Kidderminster and Wyre Forest (GR 845833).

This walk is undoubtedly one of the most spectacular in Staffordshire. Beginning in Kinver, it quickly heads for the dramatic sandstone escarpment known as Kinver Edge, originally part of a royal forest. The route follows the ridge, where there are magnificent views over a vast sweep of countryside, before returning to Kinver, visiting the church, on its fine hill-top site, on the way.

The Walk

On leaving the inn turn left and walk along the High Street as far as the Old Plough. Bear left here (signposted 'Kinver Edge'), then left again into Fairfield Drive. Follow the road to Foley Infants School and a few steps beyond it, further up the slope, you come to another road. Turn right, then immediately left at the junction. There are striking views at this point of Kinver, set amidst woods and soaring hills.

Follow the road as it climbs steadily between trees, passing various houses and bungalows which cling to the wooded

slopes. Further up, on the higher ground, you pass some public conveniences. Continue for about 60 yards until you reach a junction. Church Road is on the left. Turn right at this point and pass the National Trust sign for 'Kinver Edge'. This area is an important location for nature conservation and geology and has been designated a Site of Special Scientific Interest. Much of the woodland hereabouts is only about 50 years old and includes oak, birch, wych-elm and ash, among other species. At the turn of the century the Kinver Light Railway, which connected the village with the Midland network, helped to make Kinver Edge a renowned beauty spot and a popular destination for people from the Black Country.

As you leave the road, the path forks. Veer left and head down beside lines of birch trees. There are several seats conveniently positioned here. Descend the gentle slope, then continue towards the cover of more trees. As you reach them, swing left to join a sandy path running along the perimeter of the woodland. Beyond the fence are good views to the south-west.

Follow the path as it cuts between banks of bracken and gorse. On the right are glimpses of heathland, on the left are views of fields and woods. Pass some posts and railings and a sign – 'no overnight tents or caravans'. Just beyond the sign you come up to a junction of tracks by a large oak tree with gnarled branches. In front of you is a glorious vista, surely one of the finest in the county, a splendid patchwork of fields and trees as far as the eye can see.

Turn right and follow the wooded path between trees and banks of undergrowth. You may catch sight of scurrying squirrels and you will notice several paths leading to the locally famous cave dwellings and rock houses, some of which were inhabited until quite recently. These curious caves or grottoes were hewn out of solid sandstone. They are now in the care of the National Trust.

Follow the ridge path beyond the trig point and on this stretch there are magnificent views across to the Welsh hills, Shropshire, Worcestershire and parts of the West Midlands. Eventually, the path curves to the right by a directional marble presented by the Rotary Club of Kinver. Take the left-hand path of two parallel routes and follow it down through the undergrowth. Further down, when you reach a grass clearing, curve right and descend some steps. Follow a clear, sandy path to some steps, beyond which is the road.

Bear left and at the junction turn right. Keep the sandstone tower of Kinver church on the horizon. Follow the lane as it rises above the buildings of the village. Continue to the church and its avenue of beech trees in the churchyard. Retrace your steps down the lane and, after about 100 yards, veer half-right down the bank, following a wooded path. Join a drive, turn right and pass the entrance to Cliff Villa. When the drive peters out, continue ahead on a path, turn left and go down some steps. Follow the path between private gardens, walk along to the road and turn left. The inn is on the left.

Lower Penn
The Greyhound

The village of Lower Penn lies within a conservation area and includes a number of picturesque houses and cottages. Records prove that the Greyhound has been licensed since 1907, though the actual building dates back to the 1830s. Its gleaming white frontage is regarded as something of a local landmark. Inside, there is a cosy lounge and lounge bar.

Food is served between Monday and Sunday and large groups are asked to book in advance. The menu lists dishes such as home-made lasagne, mixed grill, minted lamb steak, Cajun chicken, steak and ale pie, battered cod, gammon steak, cheese and broccoli bake, home-made mushroom stroganoff, and several balti specialities, including chicken balti and vegetable balti. The Greyhound also offers speciality Tex Mex dishes, as well as various starters, a children's menu and a specials blackboard which always includes several steaks. In addition to a guest ale, among the beers to be found at the inn are Banks's Original and Banks's Bitter. There is also Scrumpy Jack and Woodpecker cider, Guinness, Harp lager

and Fosters. Outside is a beer garden and a play area for children. Dogs are not permitted inside the pub.
Telephone: 01902 334743.

How to get there: From Wolverhampton follow the A454 Bridgnorth road and then turn left at Wightwick Manor, heading towards Castlecroft. Cross the canal, then bear right. At the T-junction turn right, then immediately left for Lower Penn. The inn is on the right at the next junction. Alternatively, take the A449 to Spring Hill and follow the sign for Orton. Turn right, then right again and go along to the inn.

Parking: There is a car park at the pub.

Length of the walk: 3½ miles. Map: OS Landranger 139 Birmingham and surrounding area (GR 866962).

This walk follows a stretch of the Kingswinford Railway Walk before heading across the fields to join the towpath of the Staffordshire and Worcestershire Canal. The return leg rejoins the route of the old Kingswinford railway line.

The Walk
Leave the pub, turn right and pass Lower Penn Victory Hall, built by local residents in the early 1950s with the use of two army Nissen huts. The lane cuts between fields and trees. Pass a cottage on the right, go under some pylons and cross the route of the old railway at Greyhound Lane Bridge. Immediately beyond it turn right and go down the embankment. Merge with the disused line, transformed in recent years into a recreational route and known as the Kingswinford Railway Walk.

Head in a northerly direction along the old trackbed, passing through a gate and then beside the remains of Penn Halt. Continue on the railway walk as far as the next bridge and then, just beyond it, take a flight of steps on the left. Turn left and follow the road. On the left is Market Lane. Pass the turning and continue for about 70 yards until you reach a footpath on the right. Follow the field boundary, keeping the hedge on the left, towards some pylons. Pass under them and in the field corner cross into the next field. Maintain the same direction and head towards Pool Hall.

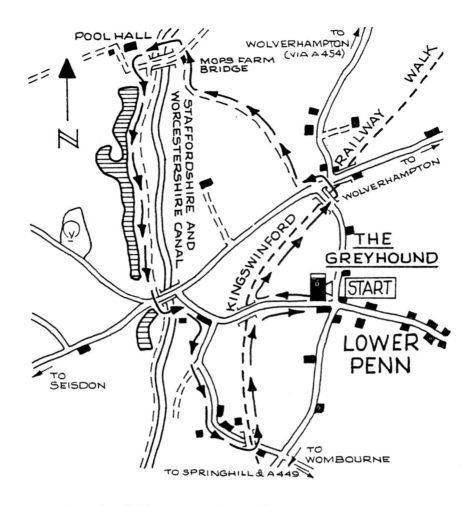

Pass into the field on your left and then continue in the same direction towards the buildings. Join a track, draw level with the house, then bear left and cross Mops Farm Bridge.

Join the towpath of the Staffordshire and Worcestershire Canal, more commonly known as the Staffs and Worcester. Financed by a local businessman and regarded as one of James Brindley's great engineering achievements, the canal, which connects the Severn with the Trent and Mersey, was completed in 1772. Follow the towpath in a southerly direction, so that the canal is on your immediate left. On the right along this stretch is a large lake. Fishermen can often be seen here.

The canal meanders between trees and undergrowth. Leave the towpath at the next road bridge – Dimmingsdale Bridge. Beyond it you can see moored narrow boats amidst the willows. Cross the bridge, then bear right into Dimmingsdale Road – signposted 'Lower Penn'. Pass a row of semi-detached houses and then turn right into Penstone Lane (signposted 'Wombourne'). Follow the road as it bends left by various dwellings and soon you reach a bridge. Just beyond it bear right and go up the embankment to rejoin the Kingswinford Railway Walk. At the top of the steps turn right and follow the old trackbed between trees and banks of undergrowth. Pass under Greyhound Lane Bridge, then turn left and head up to the road. Bear left and retrace your steps to the inn at Lower Penn.

Brewood
The Admiral Rodney

Brewood, pronounced Brood, is one of Staffordshire's largest villages and certainly one of its most picturesque. Its charming Georgian buildings and canalside setting make it a favourite choice for visitors and sightseers on summer weekends.

The Admiral Rodney has been licenced for over 100 years and until recent years it was a basic locals' hostelry. Its Victorian-style decor and furnishings still make it a popular pub in the village. Admiral Rodney was one of our great 18th century naval heroes, a man who claimed never to have lost a battle. He apparently used dried cherry stones to plan his strategy! As with Lord Nelson, it became fashionable to name inns after him.

Food is served at every session. Starters include home-made soup of the day and potato wedges with cheese and bacon. Admiral Rodney's fresh fish of the day and breaded scampi are among the fish dishes. There are also cold platters, vegetarian dishes and side orders. Among the main meat dishes are lasagne, Cajun chicken, curried meat balls, chicken and Stilton pastry parcel and a wide choice of steaks. A selection of hot and cold baguettes and hot filled jacket potatoes are also available and there is an extensive specials board. Various sweets are on offer, and a traditional Sunday lunch. Children have their own menu, which lists all the favourites. Tetley Bitter, Marston's Pedigree and a guest ale are available, as are Dry Blackthorn draught cider, Carlsberg and Stella Artois. Outside in the garden, you will find a new croquet lawn, a putting green and a summer barbecue.

Telephone: 01902 850583.

How to get there: Brewood is signed from the A449 between Wolverhampton and Stafford. The Admiral Rodney is at the southern end of the village.

Parking: The inn has its own car park. Alternatively, you can park in the village.

Length of the walk: 5¾ miles. Map: OS Landranger 127 Stafford, Telford and surrounding area (GR 884085).

There is much to see on this walk. Beginning in Brewood, once part of a royal forest, the route follows a stretch of the Staffordshire Way before reaching the gates of Chillington Hall, a historic house which is sometimes open to the public. The return leg follows the towpath of the Shropshire Union Canal.

The Walk

Emerging from the car park of the inn, turn left and walk down between rows of pretty cottages. Just beyond a development of new houses take a bridlepath on the right. This is Hyde Mill Lane. Pass a farmhouse and pond on the left and continue on the track. Cross over the line of the Shropshire Union Canal and pass a large white house on the left. At the next junction bear left towards Hyde Farm. Follow the track round to the right, passing a turning on the left and a farmhouse on the right. Continue ahead, following the route of the Staffordshire Way.

Turn left at a bend in the track and cross a stile. Follow the left-hand boundary of the field – the Staffordshire Way symbols can be seen along here. In the corner cross two stiles beside some

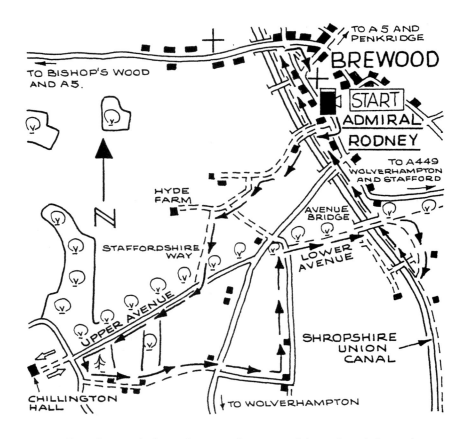

trees. Just beyond them is an oak tree, with a sign 'please keep strictly to the waymarked path when crossing the avenue'. Cross the Upper Avenue leading to Chillington Hall and look for a stile on the far side. Turn right and follow the country lane, with the avenue parallel on the right.

On reaching the next junction you will see the wrought iron gates at the entrance to Chillington Hall, the home of the Giffard family since the 12th century. The present house dates from the 18th century. The park was landscaped by 'Capability' Brown in about 1730, and in the grounds is an area known as Giffard's Cross. This is, allegedly, where Sir John Giffard killed a panther with an arrow from a crossbow. Chillington Hall is open to the public during the summer months.

If you visit the Hall, walk back down the lane, pass the road along which you came from Brewood, and continue ahead. Take the next turning on the left – a bridlepath. Pass some woodland on the left, followed by a pretty thatched cottage and a house. Several old water pumps can be seen along this stretch. Further on, the track becomes grassy and quite muddy in places. At the road junction go straight across and follow a lane between hedgerows. Swing left by The Gables and continue on the lane as it runs past oak and holly trees.

Pass several cottages and a private road on the right. Bear right just before the lane reaches a junction and follow the Lower Avenue through the trees. Eventually you reach the route of the Shropshire Union Canal. Avenue Bridge, with its fine classical design, is an impressive sight. The Giffard family believed that the waterway, canals being still regarded as a new concept at the time it was built, would create an unsightly scar on the landscape. A deep cutting and an elegant classical bridge ensured that it was concealed from view.

Beyond the bridge, swing half-right through the trees to the field corner. Bear right and follow the field edge, keeping the trees on the right. Follow a track for several steps and then go through a gate. There is a sign here – 'please shut the gate'. Make for the right-hand corner of the field, where there is a stile. Join the towpath of the Shropshire Union Canal and bear right. Ahead of you is Avenue Bridge, its graceful lines perfectly framed by trees. The arch reflected in the water adds a final touch of natural symmetry.

Follow the towpath along a pretty, peaceful stretch of the canal. Trees line the route. Pass under a road bridge and then beneath the bridge carrying the bridlepath encountered at the start of the walk. Proceed beyond the next bridge and then, at the next one, leave the towpath and bear right into Brewood. Soon the outline of Speedwell Castle, a renowned Georgian Gothic folly, comes into view on the right. Bear right in the village centre and follow the road round the corner. On the left is Brewood's fine church, with its spire of over 160 ft visible from some way off. Beyond the church you reach the inn.

4 Bishop's Wood
The Royal Oak

Bishop's Wood lies on the Staffordshire/Shropshire border and from the village there are good views over a wide area of countryside. The route of Watling Street, the famous Roman road, is about a mile to the north of the village, which was part of a private hunting reserve in the 12th century.

The Royal Oak dates from the early 18th century and was originally a staging post during the coaching era. There were stables here, where horses were changed. Its name recalls, of course, the tree in which Charles II hid in the mid 17th century. The history of the area is recorded inside the pub.

Food is served every day. You will find a specials board and an extensive range of dishes from which to choose. There are sandwiches — such as cheese, tuna, prawn, salmon, and egg mayonnaise — soup of the day, several ploughman's lunches and salads. Broccoli and mushroom mornay and vegetable moussaka are examples of the vegetarian meals. Cottage pie, breaded

scampi, sausage, egg and chips, 10 oz sirloin steak, steak and kidney pudding, haddock, cod and lasagne are other main courses. The children's menu includes beefburger and chicken nuggets. It is advisable to book beforehand for the very popular Sunday lunch. Banks's Bitter and Mild and Martston's Pedigree are available on handpump. There is also Fosters, Harp, Guinness and Scrumpy Jack cider. No dogs, please.
Telephone: 01785 840599.

How to get there: From the A5 between Cannock and Telford turn off to the south for Bishop's Wood. The Royal Oak is at the southern end of the village, on the right.

Parking: There is room to park at the pub.

Length of the walk: 3 miles. Map: OS Landranger 127 Stafford, Telford and surrounding area (GR 836094).

This walk abounds with romantic tales of royal adventure. From the inn the walk heads for Boscobel House where Charles II sought refuge from Cromwell's soldiers. On the return leg the route passes Blackladies, supposedly associated with an intriguing and unholy secret scandal involving the church.

The Walk
Emerging from the inn turn right, pass over the junction and follow the road towards Codsall. This road represents the county boundary between Staffordshire and Shropshire. Pass a pair of semi-detached houses on the right and continue on the road until you reach the entrance to Boscobel House, built about 1600. It was here that Charles II hid from Cromwell's men after being defeated by the Roundheads at the battle of Worcester in September 1651. The story suggests that he first concealed himself among the branches of a nearby oak tree. The Parliamentary troops searched the grounds of the house but apparently never lifted their eyes to look at the tree. Later, when darkness fell, Charles made his way to the house, where he hid in the attic. The following day he made his escape and travelled to the continent. He was eventually restored to the throne in 1660. Boscobel House, which is an English Heritage property, is open to the

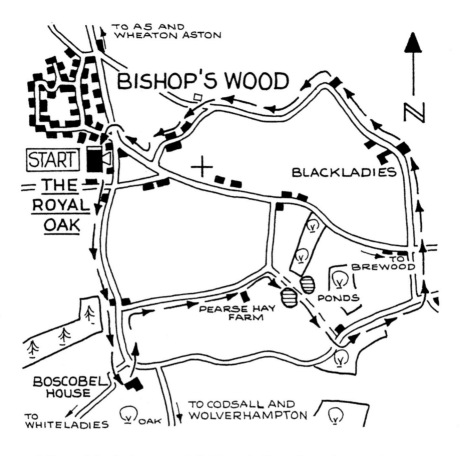

public and includes an exhibition dedicated to the royal escape.
In the nearby fields is a descendant of the original oak tree used
by Charles to hide from his enemies.

About a mile to the south-west of Boscobel House are the
remains of Whiteladies Priory, a 12th century nunnery. Charles II
was said to have also sheltered in a house near this site.

Return to the road and turn left. Bear right after a few moments
at the sign for 'Pearse Hay Farm'. Follow the track between
hedgerows. The soaring spire of Bishop's Wood church can be
seen across the fields. Continue, with views over a landscape of
gently swelling farmland. Pass some farm buildings on the right
and, when the track bends sharp left, go right and through a

wooden gate to join another track. Follow it towards some woodland and soon it cuts between two tree-fringed ponds.

Continue on the track to the road. On the corner here is Eva Cottage. Bear left and walk down beneath overhanging trees. Take the next left turning and follow the lane between hedgerows. At the junction you will see some white railings on the corner. Cross over and take the signposted drive towards Blackladies. Soon the impressive outline of the house comes into view. There was once a Benedictine priory here, established by the Bishop of Lichfield in 1130. It was later dissolved by Henry VIII and garrisoned by Cromwell's troops in 1651, whilst they searched for Charles II in the surrounding countryside. According to some sources, Blackladies has a secret passage running to Whiteladies. The story suggests that it was constructed to allow the nuns from Whiteladies to run a house of ill repute at Blackladies and to do so without arousing suspicion as to their true identity. They were said to have removed their habits in the passage as they travelled between Whiteladies and Blackladies.

Pass the main entrance to the house and follow the track as it curves to the left. Beyond the buildings of Blackladies the track cuts across country, between hedgerows and fields. Pass another farm, where there is a dilapidated old cottage among the outbuildings, and keep to the track as it bends left. Head down the slope, with the spire of Bishop's Wood church standing out among the trees. At a fork bear left and pass some more farm buildings and a timber-framed cottage. Further up the slope swing left, where you see a bridleway sign on the right. Follow the track to the road and at this point there is another very good view of the church spire.

Turn right at the road and pass a row of houses and bungalows. At the next junction bear left and the pub is a few yards along the road, on the right.

5 Derrington
The Red Lion

Derrington lies to the west of Stafford and the M6. From the village, a sizeable community, you can see the outline of Stafford Castle on the horizon.

The Red Lion opened early in the last century and has been extended over the years. Before there was running water in Derrington, villagers collected water from an old pump outside the inn. Its pleasant position on the edge of the village and its close proximity to the Stafford Newport Green Way make the pub a popular watering hole for groups of ramblers (large parties are asked to book) and for families who just want to take a short stroll in the countryside.

Food is served every day except Sunday evening. As well as a range of starters, you will find a choice of steaks – 8 oz, 16 oz, 24 oz and an amazing 32 oz – scampi, plaice, half a roast chicken, mixed grill, lasagne, chicken supreme, lamb steaks and pork chops. For something less substantial, you could choose from a selection of open sandwiches or filled crusties, with side salad and chips. There is also a soup. The children's menu includes beefburger and chips, and jumbo sausage. The inn, which has a restaurant, also offers a traditional Sunday lunch carvery and a selection of sweets. Beers on draught include Marston's Pedigree. There are four lagers – Carling Black Label, Foster's, Tennent's Pilsner and Kronenbourg. Guinness is also available, as are Dry Blackthorn and Sweet Blackthorn cider. Dogs are welcome, but in the bar only.

Telephone: 01785 242463.

How to get there: From Stafford follow the A518 west towards Newport. Cross the M6 and then turn right (signposted 'Derrington'). Drive through the village and the inn is at the far end, in Billington Lane, just before the bridge over the old railway.

Parking: There is plenty of room to park at the pub.

Length of the walk: 2¾ miles. Map: OS Landranger 127 Stafford, Telford and surrounding area (GR 888227).

This is a short and easy walk, part of which follows the route of an old, disused railway line. The return leg is along field paths and quiet country lanes.

The Walk

From the pub go to the far end of the car park and join the route of the old Stafford to Newport railway line, discontinued in 1964. It is now a recreational path, known as the Stafford-Newport Green Way. Bear left and pass under the brick road bridge. Follow the trackbed alongside Crossing Cottage, with a pretty, ornamental pond and rockery in its garden.

Continue on the path as it cuts between congested blanks of brambles, wild flowers, grass and trees. Soon the foliage thins to reveal pretty views of a farm on the right. The surrounding countryside here is mostly level farmland for as far as the eye can see. Further on, the path runs above a winding country lane. Cross the old bridge and then bear immediately right at a gap in the fence. Head down the embankment to the road and turn left.

At the next junction bear right (signposted 'Derrington'). Pass

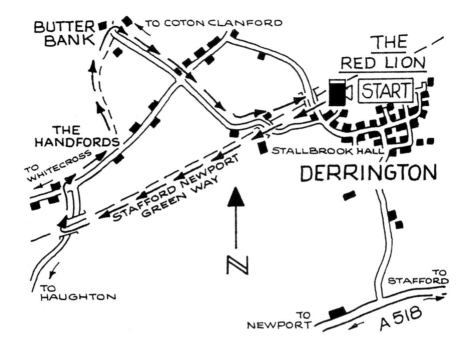

a house, Little Croft, on the right and just beyond it turn left over a stile into a field. Go straight across to a stile in the far boundary. Cross the next field by keeping the hedge line close beside you on the left. Beyond the next stile cross a wooden footbridge over an overgrown ditch. Bear right and follow the field boundary path round the corner. In the following corner cross another footbridge and keep the field boundary on the right. Farm buildings and houses are visible up ahead.

Follow the path to the corner and then keep alongside the fence until you reach a stile on the right. Cross a grassy enclosure to the next stile. On the left are views across trees and rolling fields. Go out to the lane and turn right. Walk to the junction, then continue straight ahead into Crossing Lane and follow it around several bends. At Crossing Cottage turn left and retrace your steps along the green way to the inn.

6 Norbury Junction
The Junction Inn

Norbury Junction lies on the route of the Shropshire Union Canal. The inn and a handful of houses and cottages overlook this pretty, rural spot. Less than a mile away is the larger village of Norbury.

Buit for bargees and canal workers, the Junction Inn is particularly popular in summer when the canal, which runs directly past the front of the pub, attracts armies of walkers, cyclists and boating enthusiasts. Inside are the main bar, lounge and restaurant. Outside you will find a beer garden and a children's play area.

Food is available every day. The choice of bar meals includes fish dishes, chicken, cold beef or ham, fillet, sirloin and gammon steaks, grills, light snacks and salads. There is also a specials board. The children's menu offers chicken nuggets and burgers. In the restaurant (for which booking is advisable) a carvery is available at weekends. Banks's Bitter

and Mild and Marston's Pedigree are among the real ales. Strongbow and Woodpecker are the draught ciders, while lager drinkers can choose Harp or Stella Artois. There is also Guinness.
Telephone: 01785 284288.

How to get there: From the A519 (Newcastle-under-Lyme to Newport road) turn off for Norbury, south of Eccleshall. Bear left in the village, pass the church and follow the road to the inn, which will be found on the right immediately before the canal crossing. Travelling on the A518 from Stafford, turn right at Gnosall Heath and follow the lane to Norbury Junction.

Parking: There is ample room to park at the inn.

Length of the walk: 2¾ miles. Map: OS Landranger 127 Stafford, Telford and surrounding area (GR 793228).

The outward leg of this attractive walk skirts an extensive area of woodland before joining the towpath of the Shropshire Union Canal to return to Norbury Junction along a pleasant stretch, with views of the Wrekin away to the west.

The Walk
Leave the pub by turning right and crossing the Shropshire Union Canal, or 'The Shroppie' as it is more commonly known. This is surely one of the most famous of all our inland waterways and one of the last to be built. Soon after its completion the era of the canal as a transportation network began to wane.

Pass the maintenance yard and here the scene is alive with moored narrow boats. Walk ahead along the road and on the left is the entrance to Norbury Manor. Continue down the lane towards the woodland. The canal embankment, known as Shelmore Great Bank, can be seen on the right. Follow the road between the trees. Pass a white cottage on the right. As the road bends sharp right, go straight on to follow a track running along the edge of Shelmore Wood.

Pass a gate with a sign – 'fishermen only'. Continue on the

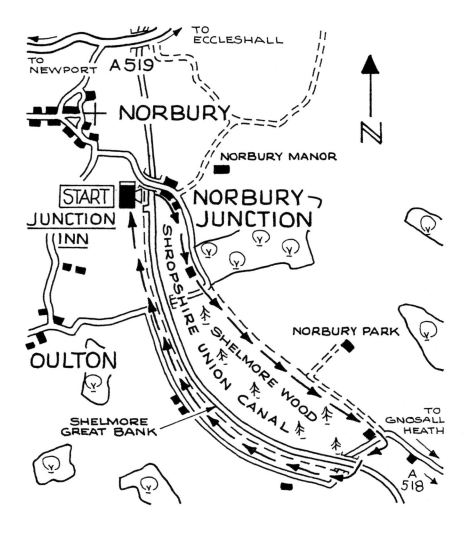

bridleway (be prepared for mud here after prolonged rain). On this stretch are young pine plantations. There are also glimpses of fields, trees and rolling countryside. Pass several ponds on the left.

Further on you join a firm track running alongside a row of oak trees on the left. The dense and extensive woodland of Shelmore Wood is still on the right. Soon you come to a junction with a concrete drive. Continue ahead, with the outline of Norbury Park on the left. Shortly you come to a brick and stone cottage by the road. Turn right and walk down through the woodland. Go through the tunnel under the canal and then bear immediately left over a stile. A flight of steps takes you to the towpath of the Shropshire Union Canal. Turn left and follow the canal along the top of the embankment.

This is Shelmore Great Bank and was built in order to avoid the route of the canal cutting through Lord Anson's estate at Norbury Park. Lord Anson was particularly anxious to ensure that the pheasants, reared for shooting, were not disturbed, and no doubt he exercised his power and influence to stop the canal from running across his land. However, the diversion was at great cost to Thomas Telford and the engineering company who built the 66-mile Shropshire Union Canal. More than once the embankment collapsed and the work was not completed until a year after Telford's death.

On the westerly horizon you will see the distinctive shape of the Wrekin, Shropshire's highest hill. According to legend, a giant who had been digging on the Welsh borders became tired and dropped his shovel here, causing a mound of earth to fall on this spot. The mound became known as the Wrekin.

Continue on the towpath, with good views of the surrounding countryside and of Shelmore Wood on the opposite bank. Pass an iron milepost and soon you reach a sign for 'Norbury Junction'. Beyond it the scene is made up of moored narrow boats clustered around the maintenance yard. Cross the stone bridge at the junction of the Shropshire Union Canal and the remains of an old disused canal to Newport. A short section is still water filled. A few yards beyond the bridge is the inn where the walk began.

7 Copmere End
The Star Inn

Copmere End is part of a chain of secluded hamlets strung along the banks of Cop Mere to the west of Eccleshall. Much of the land here belonged to the Bishops of Lichfield, whose summer residence was once at nearby Eccleshall Castle.

The Star Inn is a charming old pub, dating back over 200 years and very popular with walkers, cyclists, fishermen and visitors to nearby Cop Mere. Inside are black and white photographs of the inn, as well as of assorted village characters from down the years. Occasional auctions and various bring and buy sales take place here and the inn used to be the venue for horticultural sales. Children are welcome at the inn and there is a cosy lounge, separate from the main bar, where families will feel at home.

Food is served every day and is home cooked. A range of starters includes garlic mushrooms and melon with Parma ham and Docellate cheese. Among the main dishes are steak and mushroom pie, 12 oz steaks, T-bone steaks, lasagne, sweet and sour pork and Barnsley lamb chops. There is also a choice of

sandwiches, filled rolls, soup, ploughman's lunches and salad. Puddings include sticky toffee pudding, fruit pie and brandy fruit baskets. The Star has been a Bass pub for more than 20 years and there is Bass on handpump and several guest ales, as well as Mansfield Bitter and M&B on keg. Guinness, Carling Black Label, Stella Artois and Dry Blackthorn draught cider are also available.
Telephone: 01785 850279.

How to get there: From Stafford follow the A5013 to Eccleshall, then take the B5026. Turn left (signposted 'Copmere End') and the Star Inn is in front of you at the next junction.

Parking: The Star Inn has its own car park opposite.

Length of the walk: 2½ miles. Map: OS Landranger 127 Stafford, Telford and surrounding area (GR 804294).

Cop Mere is the focal point of this walk in the tranquil Sow valley. The lake, designated a Site of Special Scientific Interest by English Nature, is a haven for ornithologists and naturalists and includes some rare reeds and grasses. The route follows the banks of Cop Mere, where there is much to see, before heading for Walk Mill. The return leg is along the road, with excellent views of the lake between the trees.

The Walk
From the front door of the inn turn right and cross over at the junction. Take the lane towards the B5026 and now the still sheen of Cop Mere comes into view on the left between the trees. Pass over the Sow, which flows through the lake, and then bear immediately left at a ladder stile. This is known as Jacob's Ladder. There is a story that suggests a local gamekeeper hanged himself from the top of the stile. His spirit is said to haunt the surrounding countryside.
Follow the edge of a pleasant field and the sounds of wildlife on the lake may now be audible. Herons, water-rails, gossanders and sedge warblers are among the birds that frequent Cop Mere, which also has the largest colony of reed-warblers in Staffordshire.
Keep to the left boundary of the field, with glimpses of the lake

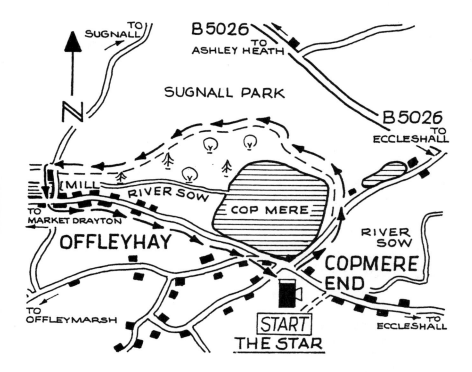

between the trees and bushes. Cross into the next field via a stile and follow the path beneath the boughs of some beech trees.

Pass a ring of trees on the right and go down to the field corner. Cross several stiles, with a patch of woodland in between and a pond on the right. Follow the wood's boundary fence, keeping it on your immediate left. Cross a stile at the corner of the trees, followed soon by another stile. The woodland is still hard by you on the left. Pass over a junction of paths and go along the edge of some beech trees. Cross another stile and then follow the right-hand edge of a field. Make for its far right corner, then go over another stile and into an elongated field bordered by trees.

The path curves a little to the right by an oak tree. Make for a gate in the next boundary and go out to the road. Turn left and walk past the remains of Walk Mill. The name comes from the process of 'walking' or 'fulling' woollen cloth to expunge extraneous natural oils. At one time the mill was used for grinding corn.

Go down to the junction and bear left. Follow the road as it cuts between the houses and cottages of Offleyhay. Beyond them the road cuts through woodland. Much of this area was originally open commonland before the Inclosure Acts. In those days Copmere End and the other hamlets were part of an extensive farming community. Grazing cattle would have been watered at the lake-side.

Soon there are glimpses of Cop Mere between the beech trees. Pass a popular viewpoint by the lake shore and return to the inn.

8 Gnosall
The Royal Oak

There is Gnosall and neighbouring Gnosall Heath – the G is silent – and the two communities are bisected by the old Stafford to Newport railway line, which was discontinued in 1964. The old line, in common with many other former railway routes around the country, has been attractively converted into a recreational path and cycleway. The Stafford to Newport Green Way, as it is known, lies just a few yards from the start of this walk.

The Royal Oak, which is located between Gnosall and Gnosall Heath, attracts a good deal of passing trade – hardly surprising as it is on the busy A518 road. Its close proximity to the Shropshire Union Canal means that it is also very popular with boating enthusiasts. The precise date of when it was built is not clear but it is understood to have been a coaching inn at one time. A weekly cattle market used to be held here every Wednesday and there are records which indicate that cattle sales took place as recently as 1934. Inside, the pub is very quaint with a cosy bar and lounge. There is also a function room.

There is a good choice of food at the Royal Oak, including a selection of starters, such as soup of the day, deep-fried Brie wedges and garlic mushrooms. Among the main courses are breaded plaice, wholetail scampi, lasagne and poacher's chicken. One of the most popular dishes is the appetising Royal Oak Grill, which consists of egg, chips, gammon, black pudding, grilled tomato, lamb chop, sausage and 5oz rump steak. There are also vegetarian dishes, cold platters, a specials board, a weekend carvery, a children's menu and a range of desserts — including the popular Royal Oak Ultimate Sweet. Tetley Bitter, Abbot Ale, Burton Ale and a guest beer are available, and there is also Calders Creamflow, Dry Blackthorn cider, Guinness, Stella Artois and Carlsberg. The Royal Oak boasts a beer garden and a children's play area. Dogs are permitted but only in the bar and on a lead. Large groups are asked to book in advance.

Telephone: 01785 822362.

How to get there: Take the A518 between Stafford and Newport. The pub is on the main road, between Gnosall and Gnosall Heath.

Parking: The inn has its own car park.

Length of the walk: 2½ miles. Map: OS Landranger 127 Stafford and Telford (GR 826204).

This short walk makes for the Stafford to Newport Green Way, following the disused, tree-lined trackbed to the Shropshire Union Canal. Beyond Cowley Tunnel, the route passes through residential Gnosall Heath before returning to the inn.

The Walk

On leaving the inn turn left along the A518, passing a fascinating illustrated framed map of Gnosall in years gone by. Old photographs of the church, the lock-up and Cowley Tunnel form part of it. Take the path on the right and follow it to the route of the Stafford to Newport Green Way. Bear left and walk along the disused track. All around you are views across to Gnosall and the

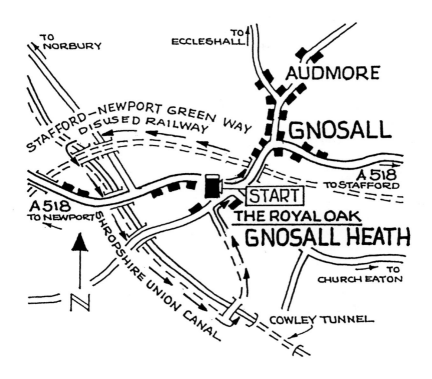

surrounding area. Looking back you can spot the tower of Gnosall's stately Church of St Lawrence, considered to be one of the finest in Staffordshire. Parts of the church date back to 1080. Huddled around it are the buildings of Gnosall village, first mentioned in the Domesday Book as 'Geneshall.'

Follow the old railway for about half a mile. Cross the Shropshire Union Canal and descend some steps to the towpath. Keep the canal on the left and walk towards the A518. Moored cabin cruisers and narrow boats can often be seen on this stretch of the waterway. The Navigation pub can be seen at the next road bridge as you continue ahead. The Boat is the next pub on the canal, seen over to the left at Pave Lane Bridge.

This inn has been in constant use since the Shropshire Union Canal, or 'The Shroppie' as it is more commonly known, was opened in the 1830s. Telford's canal, famous for its long wooded straights and deep scenic cuttings, proved to be very expensive to build and at times difficult to construct. There were frequent landslips and Telford was forced to make several costly diversions. Beyond the bridge the canal runs beside modern houses and distinctive timber chalets. Ahead now is Cowley Tunnel, hewn out of a wall of solid sandstone. The walk leaves the canal at this point but, if time allows, you may like to make a short detour and follow it through the tunnel. It is dark and dank inside; walking through it, as I did, is a curious experience.

Follow the paved path on the right, up towards the roof of the tunnel, crossing a stile leading to a track. Turn left, then left again at the next junction. Now the Shropshire Union Canal can be seen far below you, cutting through the trees. The outline of an old quarry is visible along this stretch of the walk and then the Quarry Nurseries boundary is seen on the right. Follow the path along the woodland edge and emerge from the trees by some lock-up garages. Keep to the left of the garages and go straight on at the junction, by the sign for Impstones. Follow the road through the housing estate and eventually turn right at the junction. Pass a row of striking terraced houses and continue along the road. There are various turnings on the left and right. Pass Cowley Lane on the right and return to the inn.

9 Stone
The Star

Stone, 'the canal town', expanded as a result of the coming of the Trent & Mersey Canal. Before the decline of the canal system, the waterway was the town's life-blood, helping to strengthen its local economy.

The Star is one of the town's most popular inns. Situated on the towpath of the Trent & Mersey, it attracts a lot of passing trade from both the water and the town. The pub's history can be traced back to the 16th century, though it wasn't fully licensed until 1819, many years after the canal was completed. A cannon, fired to celebrate completion of this stretch of the Trent & Mersey in the second half of the 18th century, missed its target and damaged part of the building, a bridge and one of the locks.

The pub, a charming mixture of beamed and panelled bars includes an extended restaurant and conservatory at the rear. Marton's Pedigree is available on draught and there is a guest ale, plus Banks's Mild and Bitter, Guinness, Kronenbourg and Harp. Lager drinkers may also like to try Fosters, and

Strongbow draught cider is available too. Food is served every day and the choice is extensive. There are sandwiches, soup, cold platters, mixed grill, gammon, scampi, Cajun chicken, bangers and mash, beef lasagne, steak and ale pie and various vegetarian dishes. There is a choice of several traditional Sunday roasts and a specials board. Children are welcome.

Telephone: 01785 813096.

How to get there: Stone is just off the A34 between Stafford and Stoke-on-Trent. From the A34 follow the A520 towards the town centre. The Star is on the left, just before the canal bridge. There is a British Rail station at Stone.

Parking: There is plenty of room to park at the pub.

Length of the walk: 2½ miles. Map: OS Landranger 127 Stafford, Telford and surrounding area (GR 903336).

This is a well-trodden and extremely popular trail along the banks of the Trent & Mersey to the outskirts of Stone and then back via the town centre. Much of the route provides a fascinating insight into the history of Stone and its many buildings.

The Walk

From the inn car park go through the little wicket gate to join the towpath of the Trent & Mersey at Star Lock. Turn left and follow the towpath. The buildings of Stone can be seen on the opposite bank. Pass under the bridge (number 94) and continue on the towpath. Pass the next lock and on the right are the buildings of an historic docks complex, where canal maintenance and boat building operations take place. Business is mostly very brisk, thanks to the growth of the canal as a leisure amenity.

Pass the site of the Joules Brewery. The plant is Victorian and it was here that Stone ales were produced for export to distant continents. Make for the Newcastle Road Bridge ahead and at this point you can see there is an adjoining towpath tunnel used by the boat horses. Go through the brick tunnel and continue beyond Newcastle Road Lock. This stretch of the Trent & Mersey would

have been a bustling scene at the height of the canal era, when lines of warehouses stood here. Pass beneath the route of the North Staffordshire Railway and beside Limekiln Lock. There were once several lime kilns here.

On the left is a sign for the Rising Sun public house. Pass an old milepost beside the towpath and go on to the next bridge – number 96. Ahead of you is a rural landscape of fields and hedgerows, as the towpath begins to leave the buildings of Stone and heads for open country. Leave the canal at this point and go up to the road. Cross the bridge and, as you do so, look down for a final glimpse of the Trent & Mersey and the route of the walk so far.

Follow the road beside various industrial units and make for the railway crossing. Beyond it go on up the lane to the junction. Go straight across, through the kissing gate and into Stonefield Park. Follow the faint outline of the grassy path ahead. Pass a solitary bench and, on the brow of the hill, make for a stile and gate into the next field. Once over it, turn right and the buildings of Stone immediately come into view. The park offers distant glimpses of surrounding countryside.

Head for the corner of the field and here a stile takes you into a recreation ground. Pass some swings and, at the road, bear right. On the right is the Pheasant Inn. Walk along the street, with Stone's church spire ahead. At the junction turn right into Radford Street. Cross the railway line and walk down to Granville Square.

A plane tree here replaced a pump to commemorate the Coronation of Edward VII. There is also a statue of a soldier in uniform in the square. Continue down into the High Street. Pass the ornate façade of Stone Library, then the Crown Hotel, which was a staging post on the Mail and various other coaching routes. The hotel was designed in 1779 by Henry Holland. By the early 19th century Stone had a dozen staging inns.

There is an optional detour at this point. Opposite the hotel you can stroll up Mill Street and beyond the railway bridge is Stowe Mill, where Hovis flour was patented in 1887. Return to the High Street and turn left. Stone's name is linked to the martyrdom of two Saxon princes, Wulfad and Ruffin, who were slain by their father for embracing the Christian faith. In keeping with Saxon custom, they were buried beneath a cairn of stones. A small priory was later established and around this site a small town, known then as Stanes, began to evolve. Henry III granted Stone a charter in the mid 13th century and, much later, the town grew in stature with the coming of coach travel in the 18th century and the development of Britain's canal system.

Walk down to Church Street and here you will see the entrance to St Michael's church, which includes an imposing mausoleum to Admiral John Jervis, who defeated the Spanish off the Cape St Vincent at the close of the 18th century.

With your back to the church entrance walk straight ahead, across the road and along the A520. Soon the inn comes into view.

10 Barlaston
The Duke of York

Barlaston is a large, straggling village between Stoke-on-Trent and Stafford. There is an attractive green at the eastern end of the village, around which are clustered a number of quaint old houses and cottages.

The Duke of York is a pleasantly simple village pub with various beams, horse brasses and other features commonly found in hostelries. It has a comfortable lounge and bar. The building was originally a row of cottages, the frontage dating back about 200 years. Before Bass took it over, the inn was a Bents house.

Bar meals are served every lunchtime, except Sunday. There is no food in the evening. You can choose from a specials board or the printed menu. The latter includes home-made soup, pizzas, sausage, jacket potato and beans, a bowl of chilli with jacket potato, various other filled potatoes, meat and potato pie, steak pie, pork pie and pickle, a range of oatcakes and a selection of baps. Guinness, Carling Black Label and Worthington Creamflow are all available at the inn, as well as cask Bass and

Boddington on handpump. Large groups are asked to book at weekends. Children are welcome, and dogs are allowed in the bar. Telephone: 01782 373316.

How to get there: Barlaston is signed eastwards off the A34 between Stoke-on-Trent and Stone. Cross the railway line, then turn left at the village green into Longton Road. The Duke of York is on the right. There is a railway station at Barlaston.

Parking: There is room to park at the inn. However, if the car park is busy, there are spaces in the village.

Length of the walk: 2¼ miles. Map: OS Landranger 127 Stafford, Telford and surrounding area (GR 894385).

Barlaston is closely associated with the Wedgwood Pottery and Museum. The walk is a pleasant, short stroll across the fields to the towpath of the Trent & Mersey Canal. From here you head for the Wedgwood Visitor Centre, where you can see potters and decorators at work. The route runs through the 500-acre Barlaston country estate before returning to the village.

The Walk

From the car park head down Vicarage Lane to the junction. Turn right and walk through the village. Pass Malthouse Lane on the right and continue to where the road bends sharp right. Walk ahead, signposted 'Wedgwood Visitor Centre', for several yards and then turn immediately left. Follow the path down to the bottom right-hand corner of the field, passing several oak trees. On the right are glimpses of Barlaston Hall.

Cross the stile and go straight on to the next boundary. Cross another stile and continue towards a line of trees. A lake comes into view as you descend the slope to a white gate. Trains on the nearby line can be seen from this stage of the walk. Pass through the gate and along the edge of the lake. Go through another gate and then straight ahead to a stile in the next field boundary. Follow the outline of the path towards the railway. Narrow boats on the Trent & Mersey Canal can be seen ahead.

Go through the white gate and cross the line. Wedgwood station is just a few yards down the track. Pass through another

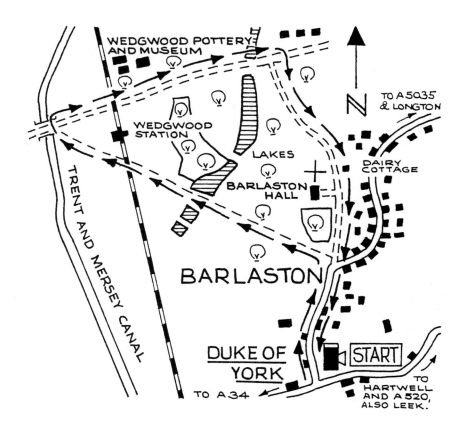

white gate and then go across the field to the road. Just a few yards away to your left is the route of the canal. The bridge here offers good views over the waterway. Do not cross the bridge – instead walk back up the road past the car park for Wedgwood employees and visitors. Recross the railway line and pass the entrances to the factory.

The Wedgwood Pottery works date back to 1759 when Josiah Wedgwood established the world famous firm. Wedgwood, the youngest of 12 children, was born at Burslem in 1730. Prior to moving to Barlaston, the original factory site was at Etruria near Stoke. The present factory was built between 1938 and 1940 and includes a model village for many of its workers.

Standing on a wooded ridge, Barlaston Hall, to the right here,

45

and its splendid landscaped parkland can be seen from some distance away. The Hall is mid 18th century and was built by an attorney from Leek. Separate from the pottery works, it has been extensively renovated and restored in recent times, but is not open to the public.

Take the next right turning (signposted 'M6' and 'A34'). Keep to the drive as it curves to the left, then the right. Soon you reach Dairy Cottage. Opposite is the lychgate to the church. Note the plaque here which reads 'this lychgate was the gift of Mary Julia Bullock who lived 30 happy light years in Barlaston and loved both the church and the village'.

Continue along the drive, with its humps, pass Barlaston Hall on the right and then walk beside lines of holly bushes, beech trees and rhododendron bushes. At the junction with the road go straight on and back to the inn.

11 Hill Chorlton
Slaters

Hill Chorlton is a small community, not far from the larger village of Baldwin's Gate and situated in the delightfully wooded, rolling country of north-west Staffordshire, close to the Cheshire border.

As a pub, Slaters has the unusual distinction of being a converted barn and still part of a working farm – Maerfield Gate Farm. It is named after the owners of the farm and was transformed in 1991 into the pub and restaurant you see today. There are various attractions – an outdoor play area and a bowling green. There is also a functions room and accommodation is available in several cottages converted from farm buildings.

Bar meals are served every day in the cosy, beamed lounge bar, where there is a wintertime fire. There is also an à la carte restaurant upstairs, open on Wednesday, Thursday, Friday and Saturday evening and Sunday lunchtime – booking advisable.

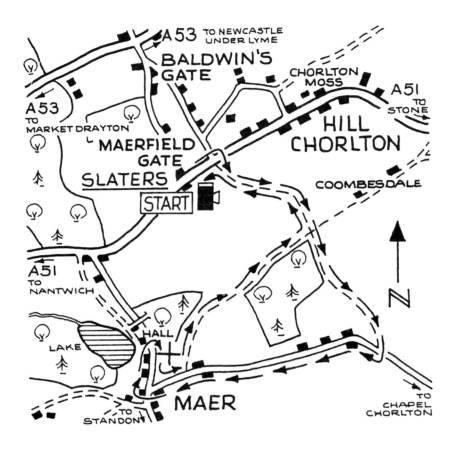

The bar menu is varied and appetising. Starters include soup of the day, pâté maison, prawn cocktail and fresh melon. Main dishes range from fried fillet of plaice and scampi to steak and kidney pie, sirloin steak and grilled gammon with egg and pineapple. In addition, there are vegetarian dishes, cold platters and various daily specials. Also available is a menu for the under eights and a traditional Sunday lunch. The beers on handpump are Marston's Pedigree and Boddingtons. Heineken, Carlsberg and Stella Artois lagers are on offer, as well as Guinness and Strongbow. Children are welcome, but no dogs please.

Telephone: 01782 680052.

How to get there: Hill Chorlton lies on the A51, between Nantwich and the A34 north of Stone. The village is just east of the junction with the A53 and Slaters will be found on the south side of the main road.

Parking: There is a spacious car park at Slaters.

Length of the walk: 2³/₄ miles. Map: OS Landranger 127 Stafford, Telford and surrounding area (GR 794393).

One of the prettiest walks in this part of the county, the route heads for the delightful conservation village of Maer. The church, perched above the rooftops of the village, is where Charles Darwin was married in January 1839.

The Walk

From Slaters turn right and walk along the main road for a few hundred yards. Pass Windclose Cottage and then turn right opposite Sandy Lane to join a footpath running along a drive. Cross a stile into a field and go forward for a few steps to the corner. Swing left and head up the slope towards some trees. Cross the field boundary and make for a stile just before the trees. From here there are far-reaching views across the tree-clad hill country of the Staffordshire/Cheshire border.

Pass into the next field, keeping the woodland on your left. Beyond the fence are the sprawling woods of Swynnerton Old Park. Make for the field corner, go through the gate and head towards the vast wooded landscape for several yards. Bear right to cross a stile. Follow the field edge, with woodland close by on the right. Just before the field corner look for a stile on the right. Cross it and turn immediately left. Head down the field boundary to another stile. Descend the steep slope and go forward to join a lightly wooded path. Be careful, as the grassy bank here can be wet and slippery after rain. Aim for another stile, where there are again impressive views over the trees of Swynnerton Old Park.

Ahead of you now on the walk are some farm buildings. Veer slightly right towards the house, then cross several stiles in fairly quick succession and go out to the road. Turn right and follow the lane between trees and hedgerows towards Maer. Pass Copeland Cottage and ahead of you now is a glorious panorama of rolling fields, woods and hedgerows, to the west and south-west.

Follow the lane and eventually it curves to the right to reveal views of Maer nestling delightfully in a hollow in the hills. Pass a footpath on the right, forming the start of the return leg of this walk, and continue down the lane into Maer. At the road junction, just beyond Maer Mews, turn right and walk along to the parish church of St Peter. The church occupies a commanding position overlooking the village and the wooded hills guarding it. It was here that Charles Darwin, the famous scientist, married the daughter of Josiah Wedgwood II. The Wedgwoods lived at Maer Hall opposite. The fine gabled house is built in the Tudor style – note the imposing arched gateway entrance by the church. The village is said to be named after the nearby mere, clearly visible from the churchyard, from which the river Tern rises to snake through the Shropshire countryside, before eventually joining the Severn.

Retrace your steps to the road junction and turn left. Pass between the buildings of Maer and then turn left at the stile, just before Primrose Cottage. Head straight up the hillside towards the trees. At this point you cannot fail to spot the sturdy old beech tree in the middle of the field, its great boughs reaching out far and wide.

Begin to veer right now and aim for the top corner of the field. Pass through a wrought iron kissing gate and follow the path ahead through the beech trees. Go between a felled tree and the remains of an upturned tree, cross into a field via a dilapidated gate and continue, with woodland on the right. On the left are glimpses of the buildings of Hill Chorlton and Baldwin's Gate.

Drop down the slope to the field corner and swing left. From here you retrace your steps along the path back to Slaters. Descend the hillside to the farm and at the road bear left. The inn will soon be reached on the left.

12 Wrinehill
The Crown

Wrinehill is a large, straggling old village on the A531 Crewe to Newcastle-under-Lyme road, about ½ mile from the Cheshire border.

The Crown used to be a coaching inn and is thought to date back about 250 years. Originally it was owned by Joules, then Bass, before the present landlord acquired it in the 1970s. Both inside and out, it is a most attractive village pub. The bar features horse brasses, beamed ceilings and cosy wintertime log fires. There is also a very pleasant family/dining area. In summer, the colourful award-winning hanging baskets and flower borders are well known and appreciated in the area.

The inn, which specialises in good quality steaks, is open every evening and both sessions at weekends. Food is available during opening hours. The imaginative menu includes 4 oz sirloin steak bap, cod and prawn bake, lasagne verdi and chicken tikka masala. There is a strong vegetarian theme and you will find the menu

offers tagliatelle nicoise – as well as other dishes. The list of sweets is tempting. Among the real ales are Worthington Best Bitter and Marston's Bitter. There are also guest beers. Lagers include Carling Black Label and Carlsberg and the cider is Dry Blackthorn. No dogs please.
Telephone: 01270 820472.

How to get there: From the A525 between Newcastle-under-Lyme and Whitchurch, join the A531 at Madeley Heath and follow the road into Wrinehill. Turn left into Den Lane and the inn is on the right.

Parking: The Crown Inn has its own car park.

Length of the walk: 2½ miles. Map: OS Landranger 118 Stoke-on-Trent and Macclesfield area (GR 753472).

Much of this walk is across open farmland to the east of the A531. The route begins by exploring the village of Wrinehill before heading for pleasant tracts of countryside, which offer spectacular views to the west beyond the Cheshire border. The standard of waymarking on this walk is very good.

The Walk

On leaving the inn turn right, pass a line of houses, then bear right at a public footpath (signposted 'Ravenshall'). Follow the field boundary down to the corner, cross a stile and then veer right and head down to a cream cottage – Fox Hollow. Cross a stile, walk along the drive and through a white gate. Follow the drive and, at the junction with a track, bear left. Pass a cottage with lattice windows, on the left. After about 60 yards you will see a waymarked path on the right. Cross the stream and follow the path – somewhat overgrown in summer. Cut between a hedgerow and fence and then pass a white cottage. At the road go straight over and follow the waymarked track.

Walk beside farm buildings and cottages – Ravenshall Farm. Continue up the track between hedgerows. As it begins to curve right, go straight on over a stile. Further on there are good views back to the rooftops of Wrinehill. The surface of nearby Betley

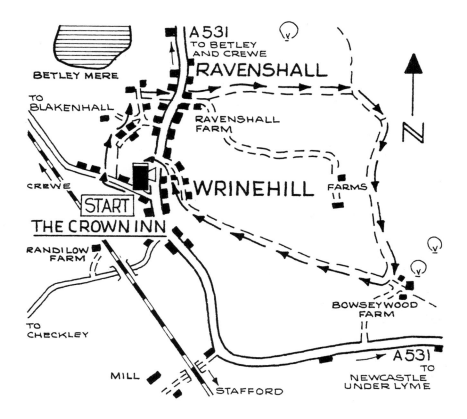

Mere can also be seen. The village of Betley was recorded in the Domesday Book and was once a market town. On the far horizon is the hazy line of the Welsh hills.

Cross the field, with the hedge line on your left. Pass through the gap into the next field and go straight across to the stile. Head straight on for the next stile. Several routes meet at this point. Cross several stiles in quick succession and then swing half-right to a double stile in the holly hedge. Walk straight ahead across the field. A farm is visible down below you in the fields to the right. There are very good views from here over distant rural landscapes.

Make for a stile in the next boundary, cross a farm track and then enter the field beyond. Cross it to a stile, then go straight down the field towards a line of trees, a fence boundary and another stile. Cross the stile, go over a grassy hump and down to the corner of the field. Look for some gates. The buildings of Bowseywood Farm are visible on the left. Cross the stile just before the farm track. Don't join the track, but instead take the stile on the right, immediately beyond the one you have just crossed. Walk straight across the field, passing under some power lines, and soon you reach a stile in the right-hand boundary. Cross it and head up the grassy hillock. Keep the field boundary on your left and look for a stile ahead. Cross into the next field and continue beside lines of trees. On the far side make for another stile and, once over it, bear immediately left by a pond. Follow the path as it keeps to the left side of the water and then cuts through the garden of a chalet bungalow. Join the drive and follow it between other properties. Beyond Maryfield Cottage bear left and go up to the main road in the centre of Wrinehill. Turn left and follow the road for about 100 yards. Cross over and veer right into Den Lane. The inn is on the right.

⓭ Rudyard
The Poachers Tavern

Rudyard is a small village located at the southern edge of Rudyard Lake, a popular venue for various leisure pursuits. Before the nearby railway closed, the village had its own station.

Until the mid 1980s the Poachers Tavern used to be known as the Station Hotel, before it reverted to its original name of Poachers. Parts of the building date back to the 17th century but much of what you see today is Victorian.

The emphasis is very much on food and the choice includes a range of interesting starters – garlic mushrooms and dovetail of melon with fresh fruits among them. Various short-crust pastry pies and pasta dishes feature as main courses, and fish is available in the form of grilled local rainbow trout, poached Scottish salmon and traditional battered cod. There is also a selection of ploughman's lunches, salads, sandwiches and vegetarian dishes, and a specials board. As for drinks, John Smiths, Old Peculier, Theakstons XB and Theakstons Mild are among the choice

of beers, and there are several lagers, including Fosters and Kronenbourg. There is Strongbow cider and hot drinks are available throughout the year. Outside is a beer garden. Dogs are also welcome at The Poachers Tavern which is closed on Sunday evening and all day Monday.
   Telephone: 01538 306294.

How to get there: Leek is the nearest town to Rudyard. From the town centre follow the A523 towards Macclesfield. After about 2 miles you turn left to join the B5331 to Rudyard. The Poachers Tavern is on the left, in the centre of the village.

Parking: There is a spacious car park at the side of the inn.

Length of the walk: 3½ miles. Map: OS Landranger 118 Stoke-on-Trent and Macclesfield area (GR 954577).

Rudyard Lake is one of north-east Staffordshire's most famous attractions. In the Victorian era it was especially popular with visitors from the Potteries. This walk heads for the lake shore and then goes along winding woodland paths, where there are tantalizing glimpses of the lake dotted with yachts and other craft. The route follows a stretch of the Staffordshire Way before heading back to Rudyard.

The Walk

Emerge from the car park and turn right. Follow the road down the hill and then bear left just before the Anglo garage. Pass through a wrought iron gate and follow a wooded path alongside a canal feeder stream. Pass over a footbridge with white railings and continue on the path beside the stream. Ahead of you is the dam of Rudyard Lake. Go through a little white gate and then follow the path as it curves to the left and up the bank. From the trees at the top there are splendid views of the water.
   Rudyard Lake is a reservoir almost 2 miles in length. It was constructed to supply water to the Trent & Mersey Canal and its delightful pastoral setting, surrounded by gently rising hills

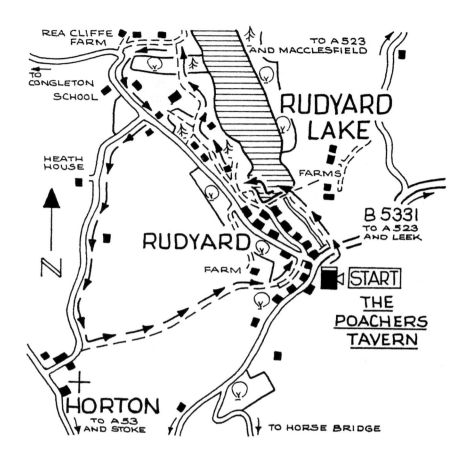

and woods, made it a fashionable resort during Queen Victoria's reign. In that age of elegance and social graces young ladies would be escorted along the woodland paths overlooking the lake, by attentive and courteous suitors. One such young man, Lockwood Kipling, proposed to his companion, Alice MacDonald, as they strolled by the water's edge in 1863. They later married and produced a son, whom they christened Rudyard in memory of their visit here. Rudyard Kipling grew up to become, of course, one of the world's most famous writers.

Join a track running along the edge of the lake and, beyond the buildings of the sailing club, veer away from the water towards the trees, where you reach a fork. Bear left here and follow the path up the bank to the road. Turn left and then immediately right (signposted 'Horton Lodge'). When the track swings right to the caravan park, continue ahead on a walled track. This is the route of the Staffordshire Way.

The track narrows to a path. Avoid a path on the left and continue between houses and stone walls. Pass The Villa and drop down the slope by the caravan park. Bear left at the Staffordshire Way sign. Follow the path through the woodland. The lake is visible on this stretch of the walk, glimpsed between lines of trees on the right. As you approach a collection of caravans, turn right and continue to follow the Staffordshire Way. The route cuts through a bracken-covered clearing to reach a junction. Bear left at this point and follow the stony track through the trees. Houses and bungalows are visible here. Emerge from the trees and continue between walls. Pass a farm on the right before the road.

Bear left at the road and pass St Michael's school on the right. Turn right for Horton and follow the lane as it twists and turns through the picturesque countryside. Just before you reach Horton, bear left to join a public footpath as the lane veers right. Cross a stile and walk ahead up the hill to another stile. Glance back here for a fine view of Horton church. Continue ahead, alongside a dry-stone wall, to a footbridge and stile. Go straight on, with the wall on your right, passing a farm over on the left. Cross several more stiles to a track and then walk straight on down to the road in the centre of Rudyard. The inn can be seen, a short distance away.

14 Upper Hulme
Ye Olde Rock Inn

Upper Hulme is a small moorland settlement lying in the shadow of The Roaches, a fascinating corner of Staffordshire with a strong, almost tangible, air of the past about it.

Ye Olde Rock Inn is understood to be about 300 years old and is a stone-built, Grade II listed building. The pub attracts a good deal of passing trade in the summer months and is particularly popular with walkers, who gather in the Hikers' Bar (large groups are asked to book in advance).

The inn, which does not open at lunchtime between Monday and Friday, has a varied menu and a specials board. There are starters, including soup of the day, garlic mushrooms and breaded pink trout, and a wide choice of main courses, for example, steak bap and chips, haddock or plaice, lasagne, steak and kidney pie, butterfly chicken breast and gammon or sirloin steak. You will also find various vegetarian dishes, a selection of sandwiches, ploughman's lunches, and salads. A children's menu offers jumbo cod, fish fingers, chicken teddies and half-size scampi. The inn

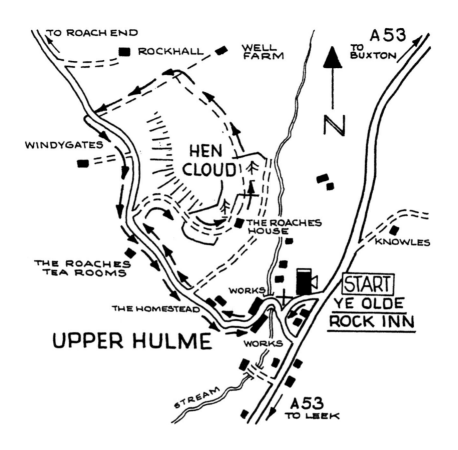

serves several lagers – Carling Black Label, Carlsberg Export, Grolsch and Castlemaine XXXX – as well as Guinness and Olde English cider. Bass is available on draught and there is also Tetley Bitter, Worthington and Calders Creamflow. Any dogs in your party can join you in the Hikers' Bar. In the summer there are tables and benches outside.

Telephone: 01538 300324.

How to get there: From Leek or Buxton follow the A53 and turn off at the sign for Upper Hulme. The inn is only a few yards from the main road.

Parking: There is a large car park at Ye Olde Rock.

Length of the walk: 2¾ miles. Map: OS Landranger 119 Buxton, Matlock and Dove Dale area (GR 014611).

Windswept expanses of heather moorland and ghostly gritstone rock formations await you on this fascinating walk around Hen Cloud, part of The Roaches, a famous chain of crags on the Staffordshire Moorlands. The views from the tops are tremendous.

The Walk

From Ye Olde Rock Inn turn right and walk down the lane towards Upper Hulme. Pass the Methodist church, dated 1838, now a holiday cottage. Further down is a lamp standard with a plaque which reads 'Harold's Lamp. In memory of the late Councillor Harold Shufflebotham.' Turn sharp right here and go down to the centre of Upper Hulme. Pass some pretty stone cottages and a weir rushing over the stones. Follow the lane round to the left and between the factory buildings of Hillcrest Engineering and Roaches Engineering. Keep to the lane as it bends to the right beyond the buildings.

The lane bends right again by some cottages. Head on up the hill away from Upper Hulme. Pass the entrance to The Homestead and then walk beside some larch trees. Suddenly the jagged outline of Hen Cloud looms into view. In misty conditions its ragged shape lends a sinister air to the surroundings. Pass alongside a line of pine trees. The views from here across the Staffordshire Moorlands are spectacular. Soon you reach The Roaches tearoom. Farmhouse breakfasts and cream teas are available here.

The road curves to the right, with Hen Cloud and The Roaches clearly visible here. Take the stony track on the right to Hen Cloud and The Roaches House. Follow the track as it swings to the right, passing beneath the gritstone outcrops of Hen Cloud. Across to the right are widespread views towards Upper Hulme. Pass between trees and clumps of bracken and enter a beech woodland. The ground here is littered with gritstone rocks and boulders, giving a fascinating insight into the geology of this crumbling, primitive landscape – a place of mystery and legend.

Soon the dark stone edifice of The Roaches House comes into view, its commanding position taking advantage of the views across the Staffordshire Moorlands. Pass to the left of the house and look for a stile in the fence. Cross it and veer right to follow a path up between the trees and outcrops. Further on, you emerge from the trees to cross the heather moorland. This land is owned by the Peak National Park and is part of a nature reserve which includes various habitats supporting a variety of wildlife.

Gradually, the path climbs to the windswept summit of Hen Cloud. From the gritstone rocks there are magnificent views to the west. At this point turn right and follow the path. The rocks are now on your left. When you see the road down below you, begin to veer to the right, following the path down through the heather. The Roaches rise dramatically in front of you. Cross a stile and go forward to a stile in the next boundary. Turn left and follow the path down to the road. On the right you can see the outline of a house nestling under the protective bastion of crags. As you reach the road you can see the sheen of Tittesworth Reservoir. Turn left and follow the lane all the way back to Upper Hulme. The road is rarely very busy, except perhaps sometimes in summer and on bank holiday weekends. On reaching Upper Hulme walk up to the junction and bear left. The inn is on the left.

15 Hulme End
The Manifold Valley Hotel

Hulme End, in the Manifold valley, is surrounded by some of the finest scenery in the Peak District National Park. It is a remote community, with a shop and a handful of houses and cottages.

The Manifold Valley Hotel, situated on the banks of the river Manifold, is built of mellow stone and thought to be about 300 years old. It was originally known as the Light Railway Hotel, in the days when this isolated valley echoed to the sound of steam trains on the now disused track nearby.

Inside the extensively refurbished former coaching inn there is a dining room and a welcoming lounge bar. You will find outside seating at the front and rear. There are always three cask beers which might include Marston's Pedigree and Mansfield. There is also Strongbow cider, Guinness, Kronenbourg and Heineken. Food is served every day and the menu changes constantly. Among the starters you may find on offer are chicken liver pâté, prawn cocktail, leek and potato soup and smoked trout. Examples of main courses are scampi, rigatoni bolognaise, marinated chicken breast, gammon steak, traditional steak and ale pie, fillet

steak and leek and Stilton bake. An all day breakfast is also served, and there is a choice of sandwiches with various fillings. The children's menu offers sausages, fish fingers, chicken nuggets and chicken teddies. A selection of sweets is available and the inn offers en suite bed and breakfast accommodation. No dogs please.
Telephone: 01298 84537.

How to get there: Hulme End is near Hartington. From Ashbourne follow the A515 north towards Buxton. Turn left at the sign for Hartington and follow the B5054 through the village and on to Hulme End. The inn is on the left. From Leek take the A523 towards Ashbourne. Bear left onto the B5053, then join the B5054 just north of Warslow, to find the inn on the right.

Parking: There is a car park at the rear of the hotel. If it is busy, you can park at the public car park located along the main B5054 towards Warslow.

Length of the walk: 2¼ miles. Map: OS Landranger 119 Buxton, Matlock and Dove Dale area (GR 106593).

From the hotel this short walk heads south to Ecton before following the valley floor back to Hulme End. The Manifold, which rises near Buxton, is rarely out of sight on this charming route, with its stunning views of the southern Peak District. The river flows prettily through a deep gorge and in places is known to disappear down 'swallet' holes in the limestone, so that above ground all you see is a dry watercourse.

The Walk

From the inn turn left and take the road on the left, immediately before the bridge. Follow the road, with the meandering Manifold river parallel on the right. Pass a turning to Beresford Dale and continue. Take the next right turning – signposted 'Ecton' and 'Butterton'. There is a glorious view of the Manifold valley at this point, the Derbyshire and Staffordshire hills and moorland of the Peak District unfolding before you.

Pass the entrance to a stone house and look for a stile just beyond it in the left-hand boundary. Cross the field, keeping the house over on the left. Make for a gate and a gap stile ahead of you

in the boundary ahead. Cross the next field by heading diagonally right to another stile by a stone cottage. In the next field continue diagonally to a little scurrying beck and a stile in the far corner. Turn right and follow the lane, passing a red telephone box and a cottage. At the next junction, in Ecton, bear left. The lane runs alongside the Manifold and under the dramatic cliffs of Apes Tor, a rock face in the gorge of the river. As a geological feature, it is fascinating, illustrating the various faulting and folding processes that have helped to shape this magical landscape.

At the next junction bear right for several yards, then right again to join the route of the Manifold Way. This follows the old Leek and Manifold Valley Light Railway, a narrow gauge railway which drew railway supporters and visitors from far and wide. The railway closed in 1934 and the lines were removed just before the Second World War. The trains may have gone but these days the old trackbed is a popular walking and cycle route.

The way crosses the Manifold a little further on. Apes Tor rises in dramatic fashion over to the right. Cross an old bridge on the embankment and soon you reach the parking area by the road. Walk though the car park to the road and bear right. Pass another red telephone box and follow the road past Hulme End village stores. Soon you are back at the inn. If time allows, have a look at the nearby visitor centre, based at Hulme End's old railway station, which illustrates the history of the local railway.

16 Denford
The Hollybush Inn

Denford is a small village just outside Leek. It is a popular place, its pretty canalside setting attracting many walkers and boating enthusiasts.

The Hollybush Inn is a 17th century former flint mill. Its interior is cosy and inviting – you can have a drink in the main bar, with its tiled floor (and cosy fire in winter), or dine in the attractive conservatory, just a few yards from the Caldon Canal. In summer, when it is open all day, the inn can get very busy, so it is advisable to book if you are intending to have a meal. Food is available every day, and all day on Saturday and Sunday. The pub also provides accommodation. There is a beer garden and play area outside and children are welcome.

The resident chef produces meals fresh to order. Starters include home-made soup, chicken, liver and brandy pâté, garlic bread, prawn cocktail and garlic mushrooms. Among the grills are sirloin steak, gammon steak, T-bone steak and lamb chops. Other main dishes are chicken tikka, garlic chicken and mushrooms, battered cod, beef in beer casserole, breaded plaice and scampi and steak and mushroom pie. Liquid choices include several lagers – among them are Carling Black Label, Kronenbourg and Pilsner Urquell. There is Strongbow cider, Guinness, John Smith's Bitter on keg, and a good selection of draught ales, including Theakston Mild and guest beers. Dogs are welcome, but in the bar only please.

Telephone: 01538 371819.

How to get there: Denford lies south of the A53 between Leek and Newcastle-under-Lyme. A mile or so from the outskirts of Leek, take the turn off for Denford and drive as far as the canal bridge. The inn is just before it on the right.

Parking: There is room to park at the pub.

Length of the walk: 3½ miles. Map: OS Landranger 118 Stoke-on-Trent and Macclesfield area (GR 955535).

Beyond the Caldon Canal this ramble of varied delights cuts across country to the village of Cheddleton where there is the opportunity to visit a flint mill. From here the walk returns to Denford by following the calm waters of the canal. Passing narrow boats are part of the charming scene here.

The Walk
Emerge from the pub car park and turn right to cross the Caldon Canal. Follow the lane between banks and hedgerows and soon it begins to twist and turn. When the lane eventually bends sharp right, go straight up the bank to join a track. Follow it to the left of a house. Soon the muddy track begins to venture out across open farmland. Cross a stile by a gate and then join a firm farm track on a bend. Go straight ahead, passing a cottage on the right. Walk along to the entrance to Lee House Cottage and bear left. Cross a cattle grid and after several yards swing left – signposted 'Cheddleton'.

Make for the corner of the field and bear right. Head for the next corner, keeping the woodland on your left. Cross the stile and then descend between trees. The path can be quite slippery here at times. At the bottom, cross the footbridge and then

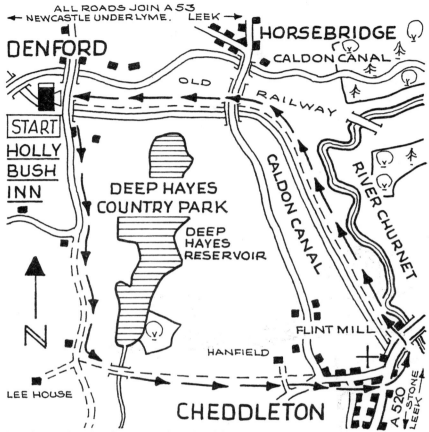

ALL ROADS JOIN A53
← NEWCASTLE UNDER LYME.   LEEK →

DENFORD

HORSEBRIDGE

CALDON CANAL

OLD RAILWAY

START

HOLLY BUSH INN

DEEP HAYES COUNTRY PARK

DEEP HAYES RESERVOIR

CALDON CANAL

RIVER CHURNET

N

FLINT MILL

HANFIELD

LEE HOUSE

CHEDDLETON

A520 STONE LEEK

head up the bank towards Cheddleton. There is a fence on the left. Cross another stile, bear right and then left. Climb steadily through the trees and beyond the next stile you go straight across a field towards farm buildings. Make for the next stile, then follow a farm track between hedgerows for a few yards.

Continue ahead under some power lines, cross a stile and then veer right, following the waymarkers for Deep Hayes. Cross the next stile and go diagonally over the field to a stone stile. Turn left and head down to the next boundary. Cross a footbridge into the next field and then follow the route alongside a line of ancient beech trees. As you draw level with the trees, begin to veer obliquely right to a stile in the stone wall.

Cross the next field and ahead of you now are views of Cheddleton and its church tower standing out plainly against a backdrop of hills. Look for the stile in the boundary, go over a track and into the next field. Cross it to the road and walk ahead into the village of Cheddleton. Pass the community centre and Ostlers Lane. On the left is the entrance to the church, dedicated to St Edward the Confessor. The church wall facing the Black Lion Inn includes the old village stocks.

Pass the inn and continue down the lane to the main A520. Turn left and go over the Caldon Canal. Bear left at the entrance to Cheddleton Flint Mill. The mill, which lies between the canal and the river Churnet, dates from the second half of the 18th century and in recent years has been fully restored. Two undershot wheels were turned by the millrace in order to grind flint powder, which was then transported by barge to the Potteries where it became an important ingredient in the production of ceramics. Cheddleton Flint Mill is open to the public at certain times and is widely acknowledged as one of the county's best-known and most popular tourist attractions.

Follow the towpath away from Cheddleton, keeping the water on your immediate left. The canal is a little over 17 miles long and was constructed in the late 18th century. Feeding into the Trent & Mersey at Etruria, it was built to enable raw materials to be transported to the nearby Potteries and beyond. The beginning of the railway age finally killed it off and by the middle of this century it was in a very sorry state of repair. However, local volunteers and canal enthusiasts formed a society, whose aim was to restore the Caldon Canal. By the mid 1970s the canal was navigable once more.

As you follow the towpath you can see the Churnet close by on the right. Pass under the stone bridge and continue on the towpath. Beyond some houses you reach another bridge. Keep on the towpath and on the opposite bank you can see the trees of Deep Hayes Country Park. The buildings of Denford soon come into view ahead. Join the road by the entrance to the Hollybush Inn.

17 Onecote
The Jervis Arms

Onecote lies on the river Hamps, a pleasant Peakland village straddling the B5053 road.

The Jervis Arms is a popular 17th century inn with an attractive waterside beer garden. From the car park a footbridge crosses the river to the pub. There are several bars and a dining room. Food is served every day and, in addition to a daily specials board, there is a printed menu and a traditional Sunday roast. Starters include soup, prawn cocktail, egg mayonnaise and potato skins. Among the main courses are prawn salad, breaded scampi, 8 oz grilled fillet, 20 oz T-bone steak, chicken fillets in Stilton, lasagne verdi, topside of beef and home-made pies. There are different flavoured jacket potatoes, ploughman's and farmer's lunches, and a varied selection of vegetarian meals – including leek and mushroom crumble, ricotta and cheese canneloni and vegetarian chilli. Beefburgers, scampi, fish fingers, sausages and egg, chips and beans provide the choice on the children's menu. There is also a good selection of sweets. Beer drinkers can

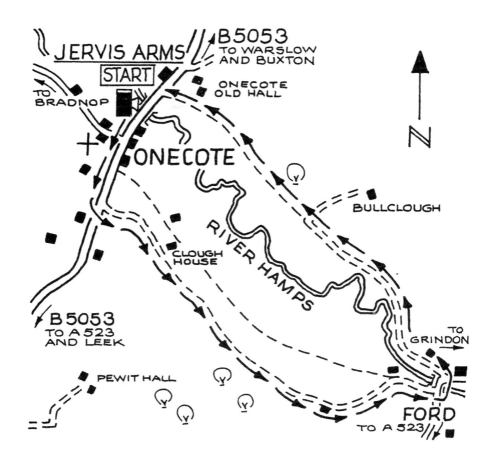

choose from draught Bass, Greene King IPA, various Titanic beers and guest ales. Carling Black Label and Tenents Extra are among the lagers. Blackthorn Cidermaster and Red Sea are the draught ciders. Accommodation is available in a converted barn adjoining the beer garden. Large groups are advised to book. No dogs please.

Telephone: 01538 304206.

How to get there: Onecote lies north of the A523 between Leek and Ashbourne. Turn onto the B5053. Onecote will be reached after about one mile.

Parking: The Jervis Arms has its own car park. The landlord requests that people knock on the inn's back door or telephone beforehand, should they wish to leave a vehicle in the car park when the pub is closed.

Length of the walk: 3 miles. Map: OS Landranger 119 Buxton, Matlock and Dove Dale area (GR 050552).

This charming valley walk keeps close to the unfledged Hamps and offers memorable views across the Peaks. The tiny settlement of Ford represents the route's halfway point.

The Walk

Leave the pub and turn right. Pass a turning to the little mid-18th century Georgian church. Continue on the main road, alongside some stone cottages. Ignore a footpath on the left and walk along the road until you reach a tarmac lane on the left, just beyond the 40 mph speed restriction sign. Follow the lane as it swings to the left, then the right. There are striking views along here of the Staffordshire Moorlands and the countryside of the upper Hamps valley.

Ascend the slope and then drop down to Clough House. Continue on to the farm, passing farm outbuildings. The track here can be waterlogged, so be prepared for mud at times. Head out across the windswept fields and on this stretch are the remains of an old stone byre. Beyond the next gate follow the track to another gate and a stile. There is a stone wall on your left. Follow the path between lines of trees and up ahead a house creeps into view. The route of the walk heads down the drive beside the house. Pass some farm buildings. Beyond them the drive curves to the right. The Hamps can be seen down below, amidst the trees.

At the road turn left, cross the river and then bear immediately left. Ford is a remote community of just a handful of old stone cottages. Keep to the left of some old barns converted into houses. The river lies over to the left. Walk almost as far as the wall and then bear right by the corner of an old barn. Cross a stile by some farm buildings and then turn left. Follow a waymarked track between wire fences, avoiding a track running off to the north, and keep to it as it cuts through the valley.

Go through a gate and continue, with the river close by you on the left. Soon another track joins our route from the left. Continue ahead, cross a cattle grid and then, as the track curves to the right to Bullclough, go straight ahead. Keep the fence beside you, on the right. Follow the path along the top of the bank and as you approach some trees, drop down to a little stream running through the fields. Once across it, bear right to a stile in the field boundary. Follow the path ahead across the field, which can be wet and spongy.

Pass under some power cables and ahead of you are the buildings of Onecote. Make for a stile by a white post. Cross it and then keep to the right of a line of power cables, aiming for a smattering of trees up on a grassy knoll. Further on, make for the right of the fence and go up the bank towards the trees. Go beyond them to the corner and cross the boundary into the next field. Head for the far boundary, where there is a stile. At the road turn left and return to the inn.

18 Wetton
Ye Olde Royal Oak

Wetton is one of Staffordshire's loneliest villages, not that its residents mind that. Its setting high in the limestone hills of the southern Peak· District makes it a perfect place in which to live. Not surprisingly, it is also very popular with tourists and walkers, particularly in the summer months.

Ye Olde Royal Oak is a classic 300-year-old inn with white stone walls and shutters and a cosy, inviting atmosphere inside. The pub is famous for being the home of the world toe wrestling championships, an event which has featured prominently in the press and on national television.

Food is served every day and includes several starters, with soup of the day being a popular choice in winter. Among the main courses are ham with egg, lasagne, steak and Guinness pie, scampi, T-bone steak and omelette. There are vegetarian meals, various sandwiches, jacket potatoes, salads and ploughman's lunches. Children's meals are also available and there is a selection of sweets and a traditional Sunday roast. As well as offering more than 30 single malts, the inn features several beers on handpump – Ruddles County, Marston's Pedigree and Black Sheep Special among them. For those who drink lager, there is Stella Artois, Carling Black Label and Heineken; Guinness and Dry Blackthorn cider are also available.

Ye Olde Royal Oak offers accommodation in four en suite bedrooms and there is a sun lounge overlooking the beer garden at the rear. No dogs please.

Telephone: 01335 310287.

How to get there: From Leek or Ashbourne follow the A523 and join the B5053 north towards Buxton. Pass through the village of Onecote and bear right, signposted Grindon. Drive through the village, follow narrow lanes and cross the Manifold. Take the next left for Wetton and the public car park is on the left. To reach the pub, walk along the road and turn left at the junction to find the inn on your left.

Parking: As the pub gets very busy, the landlord requests that people use the public car park on the edge of the village.

Length of the walk: 5¾ miles. Map: OS Landranger 119 Buxton, Matlock and Dove Dale (inn GR 108554).

This is a lovely figure of eight walk through the beautiful Manifold valley, linking the villages of Wetton and Grindon. The views over rolling limestone country are stunning, especially from the entrance to Thor's Cave. Beyond the cave, the walk follows a stretch of the Manifold Way beside the meandering river. The willow warbler can sometimes be heard and the purple orchid adds a touch of colour in the summer.

The Walk

From the pub turn left and follow the village street round to the left. Pass the 19th century church and several footpath signs on the left and continue along the street between limestone cottages. Veer right at the next junction and now you are faced with a choice. To visit Thor's Cave take the signposted concessionary track and follow it across the fields. Further on you join a path, slippery at times, which takes you to the cave entrance at the top of some steps.

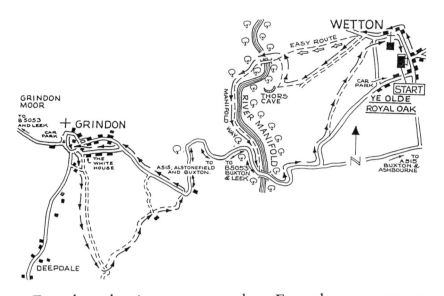

From here the views are tremendous. From the cave entrance, walk down to the bottom of the steps, taking care as you go, and bear left at the fork. Follow the path down through the trees and eventually you come down to a footbridge over the River Manifold. Cross over, look up to see Thor's Cave looming above you and then turn left to join the Manifold Way.

To avoid the cave, pass the concessionary track on the outskirts of Wetton and walk down the lane for a few yards until you reach a waymarked path on the left (Thor's Cave half a mile). Take the path and ahead of you are magnificent views of the Manifold valley, a majestic landscape of rolling green hills and limestone dales. Follow the path down the field, pass through a gap in the boundary and continue descending the slope towards some trees and bushes. Make for the bottom boundary and join a path running through the woodland. The path can be wet and very slippery in places. Pass a signposted path on the left, climbing steeply to Thor's Cave, and keep going through the trees.

Cross the Manifold river and then turn left to join the Manifold Way. The track follows the route of the old Leek and Manifold Valley Light Railway. Keep parallel to the river which may at times be no more than a dry river-bed. Keep to the route as it snakes through the valley and eventually you reach a parking area just before the road.

Bear right at the road and follow it up to the hill-top village of Grindon. Make for the Cavalier Inn and then follow the road to the left, passing the bus shelter, post box and telephone box. Bear right at the sign for the White House. Follow the track between drystone walls and over to the left are glorious views of the deep-set, limestone Manifold valley. Pass an old byre on the left and continue on the track. Pass another barn and a gate and go down the field slope to the next gate. Swing sharp left immediately before it and begin to follow the right-hand edge of the field. You are now on a stretch of bridleway, with a drystone wall on your right.

At the end of the wall, continue half-right towards the steep-sided valley. Make for a line of trees and bushes and to the left of them is a gate and stile. In the next field, continue ahead, with the wall on your immediate right. Go through a gap into the next field, still keeping the boundary wall on the right. In the bottom corner of the field is a gate into the next field. Head diagonally right now, making for a barn in the distance. Aim for the left of the bar, cross a track and drop down the slope towards the wall over on the left. After several moments a wooden gate edges into view. Go through it and up the slope to another gate. Continue ahead, with the stone wall on the right. Follow it to the field corner, then go out to the road.

Turn right and follow the lane round several bends to the Manifold. Climb steeply round several more bends to reach the higher ground, pass a footpath, cross a cattle-grid and take the next left turning. Follow the lane, pass the sign for Wetton, then a footpath on the left and keep to the lane as it curves round to the right. At this point look for a stile in the left boundary. Veer half-right across the field and make for an opening in the wall. Go straight across to a step-stile in the next boundary, then diagonally left in the next field to the far corner where there is a choice of tracks. Take the concrete one on the left and keep to the left of some farm outbuildings. Cross a step-stile and continue on the track to the road. To visit the pub, turn left, then right and walk along the village street. To return to the car park, turn right and walk along to the junction. The car park is on the left.

Alstonefield
The George

19

Alstonefield is a quiet village, situated amid the splendid limestone uplands of the southern Peak District.

The George is a solid, 16th century, stone inn, with a fine reputation. People travel from far and wide to visit the pub, which is particularly popular with Peakland walkers. It is, perhaps, advisable for large groups to book. Inside the quaint old bar the walls are adorned with photographs and prints of Staffordshire and Derbyshire scenes, and on the beams above you are scores of foreign banknotes. There is also a box of greeting cards produced by a local artist.

Among the real ales on handpump are Burtonwood Bitter and Top Hat. Dry Blackthorn draught cider, Guinness, Carling Black Label and Carlsberg Export are also served. Food is available every day and dishes include soup, chicken, chips and peas, smoked trout, lasagne, meat and potato pie, Spanish quiche, fillet steak, ploughman's lunch — with a choice of home-made liver pâté, home-baked ham, Stilton, blue Brie and Cheddar cheese — various

sandwiches and a selection of puddings, among them banana split, vanilla ice-cream and fudge and walnut pie. There is a spacious family dining room and orders for food are taken at the kitchen door. No dogs please.
Telephone: 01335 310205.

How to get there: From Ashbourne, just over the county boundary in Derbyshire, follow the A515 towards Buxton and then turn off at the sign for Alstonefield. Bear left in the village centre and the inn is on the right.

Parking: The pub has its own car park. Alternatively, you could park in the village.

Length of the walk: 3¼ miles. Map: OS Landranger 119 Buxton, Matlock and Dove Dale area (GR 132555).

The views across the White Peak region are constant and spectacular on this scenic walk in the southern Peak District. Beginning on high ground, the route makes for the banks of the delightful Dove, following the twisting river through one of Britain's most popular National Parks. This area was a favourite haunt of Izaak Walton, renowned as the author of 'The Compleat Angler'.

The Walk

From the inn turn left and then right at the next junction – signposted 'Lode Mill' and 'Ashbourne'. Pass the old Wesleyan chapel, dated 1879. Follow the lane across the magnificent high-level country of the Staffordshire/Derbyshire borders. The rolling hills are criss-crossed by the ancient dry-stone walls so characteristic of this area. Pass a footpath sign on the left, followed by the speed derestriction sign. Just beyond a copse take the waymarked track on the left. The track is about 150 yards from the first signposted path.

Walk past several stone byres on the left. The track narrows to a path between dry-stone walls, with excellent views over this high ground. Pass some more byres (the path here can become muddy after rain).

Follow the path as it bends right and left. Ahead of you is the

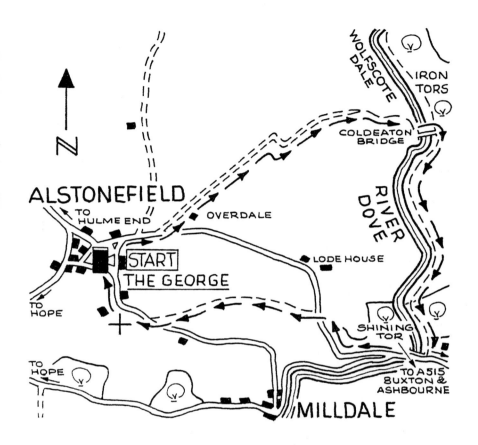

southern edge of Wolfscote Dale, through which the Dove flows. The path begins to drop down towards the wooded gorge. At the next stile swing half-right at the National Trust sign and descend the steep hillside into the gorge. The outline of the path is visible, weaving its way down the grassy bank to a footbridge over the tumbling Dove, so beloved of Izaak Walton.

Cross the bridge and then bear right. Follow the Derbyshire bank of the Dove, keeping to the clear path as it runs under the flank of soaring green hills and between lines of trees. Cross a number of squeeze stiles. The furious torrent of the river is hard by you on the right. Follow the path all the way to the next stone road bridge. Join the road, bear right and at the junction take the turning for Alstonefield, recrossing the county boundary into Staffordshire. The lane climbs steadily through the trees.

Follow the road as it curves right and begin to look for a stone stile on the left. Go up the steep, grassy slope to a stile in the top boundary. Head straight on, with the dilapidated stone wall on your left. Make for the next stone stile and go straight on across the higher ground, with the wall on your left. Cross another ladder stile in the field corner. Pass a dip in the ground and then bear left into the adjoining field. Veer diagonally right to a gap stile in the boundary wall. Cross the field to the next boundary, where there is another gap stile. Follow a wide, grassy path between dry-stone walls and maintain the same direction across the next two fields. Ahead of you is the tower of Alstonefield church, a useful landmark. In the field just before the church, go straight across to the stone stile and out to the lane. Turn right and walk alongside the churchyard. The church dates back to the time of the Normans. Soon the inn comes into view, in the centre of Alstonefield.

20 Ipstones
The Old Red Lion

Ipstones lies in the breezy country of the Staffordshire Moorlands. Clinging to the upper slopes of the Churnet valley, the village has several listed buildings. One or two local farmhouses here are reputed to have secret passages leading to the church. The Old Red Lion is one of the oldest buildings. Built about 1757, it was originally a coaching inn, with its own stables, when the old road ran past the front of the pub. James Brindley, who built the nearby Caldon Canal, was brought here when he became ill with pneumonia. He died a few days later. Immediately prior to his illness, Brindley had been surveying the canal's terminus. The work was later completed by John Rennie.

Inside the pub are several black and white photographs. One is of the inn taken in 1920, the other shows local foresters pictured outside the pub at the turn of the century. Food is available every day, except Monday and Tuesday lunchtime, though large groups can be accommodated then by prior arrangement. Dishes are served in the main bar and dining area. Bar snacks include

a range of sandwiches, soup of the day and a choice of filled jacket potatoes. Among the main meals are cod in batter, breaded scampi, 16 oz steak, 8 oz rump steak, gammon steak, curry dishes and large filled Yorkshire pudding. There is also a choice of sweets. The beers on handpump include Theakston Mild and Directors. You will also find Scrumpy Jack cider and Fosters lager. Children and well-behaved dogs are welcome. There is a beer garden.
Telephone: 01538 266345.

How to get there: Ipstones lies south of the A523 between Leek and Ashbourne. Turn off on the B5053 towards Ipstones and Froghall. The inn is on the right in the village.

Parking: There is a spacious car park at the front of the pub.

Length of the walk: 4 miles. Map: OS Landranger 119 Buxton, Matlock and Dove Dale area (GR 018497).

From Ipstones, 800 ft above sea level, the walk heads west and then south to join the towpath of the Caldon Canal. During the walk you pass another fine pub – the Black Lion, overlooking the canal, is one of Staffordshire's most inaccessible pubs and certainly one of its least spoilt. It is a true gem of a place, and certainly an ideal spot for a short break on this delightful walk. The route climbs the wooded slopes of the Churnet valley before crossing open farmland near Ipstones.

The Walk
Leave the pub, bear right and walk down the road for a few yards. Turn right (signposted 'Cheddleton' and 'Basford') and follow the lane, with good views across the Churnet valley. Further on, the lane zig-zags down through the trees and, when you reach a stone bridge, bear left immediately beyond it to join a path leading to Consall Forge.

Cross a gushing stream and pass the remains of an old stone plinth. After about 50 yards the path veers away from the stream and runs up the bank. Pass a sign 'Belmont Hall – private property

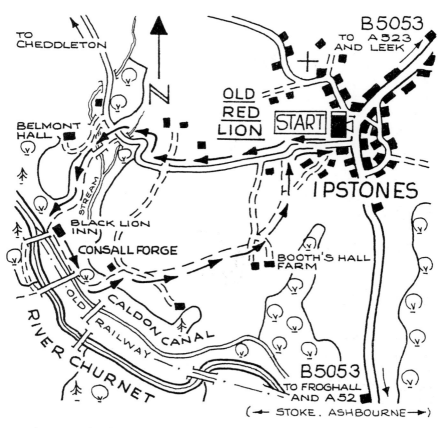

– dogs on leads – public footpath'. At the top of the steps turn left, pass a turning and follow the drive as it curves to the right. About 50 yards before the imposing entrance to Belmont Hall, veer to the left and follow a waymarked path into the corner of the field. Continue ahead, keeping to its left-hand boundary. Pass alongside some holly bushes, cross a stile and join a path running along the edge of the woodland, with the field now close by you on the right. Follow the path through the trees and after several minutes you come to a flight of steps taking you down into the wooded valley.

At the foot of the steps continue on the path and soon you are approaching the back of the Black Lion Inn. This pub, with its old-fashioned decor and lack of pretension, has a timeless appeal about it. I first called there many years ago and, since that visit, little if anything has changed. Walkers with muddy boots are welcome!

From the front door of the inn turn left and go down to the canal towpath. Consall Forge lies in a bowl enclosed by semi-natural woodland. Ash is the most common species here, with some alder, oak, wych-elm and hazel. Consall sprang into existence as the result of a water-powered ironworks. From here iron bars were then carried on mules to nearby Oakamoor to be converted into tin plate. You can see the river Churnet and the Caldon Canal running parallel, with the route of the old North Staffordshire Railway also clearly defined.

Follow the towpath, with the old line parallel on the right, and soon a row of Victorian cottages comes into view. Pass under the next bridge, then bear immediately left to climb up the bank to a track where there is a sign – 'Rough Knipe Walk and Booth's Wood Walk'. Go straight across the track and up a flight of steps in front of you. Climb the steps through the trees and, on the higher ground, you pass between carpets of bracken. Soon fields appear on the left, just before the path begins to descend to a handrail.

Veer left to a stile and into a field. Go straight ahead, with the hedge line on your left. In the corner pass through a gate by a farm. Join a track and walk down to the farm outbuildings. Turn right here, following the waymarker. Just beyond a gate, swing obliquely left, away from the track, and up ahead is a telegraph pole with several waymarkers. Veer away from the hedgerow and keep in line with the row of poles running across the field, until you see a waymarker post on the left. Make for a stile beside two gates. Veer right and walk along the field boundary towards the farm. Just before it you reach a major junction of paths. Turn left and walk along the main farm track.

When you reach a track running off sharp right to Booth's Farm, go diagonally right, across the field to the right of the track. Pass under some power lines and make for a gap in the hedgerow. Cross the next field, heading for a gap in the hedge close to the top right-hand corner. Walk straight ahead up the field – the buildings of Ipstones are visible to the right. Make for the gap stile, then head for the road. Turn right and at the junction in Ipstones bear left. The inn is on the left.

Ellastone
The Duncombe Arms

Ellastone is a large village on the north bank of the Dove. The novelist George Eliot – Mary Ann Evans in reality – chose it as the setting or Hayslope in *Adam Bede*. Staffordshire is Loamshire in the book and the magical Dove Dale is Eagledale. Readers of the classic novel can tour the area, speculating as to precisely how much the fictional village is based on Ellastone and how much springs from the author's brilliant imagination. Much of the real village is portrayed in the book and even today you can feel the presence of 'George Eliot' in Ellastone's old streets and among its buildings. The author had a great affection for the place and several members of her family lived here.

The Duncombe Arms is named after Sir Charles Duncombe, who was Lord of the Manor here at one time. He later fell on hard times and his old home has long gone. The inn – George Eliot's Donnithorne Arms – dates back to 1640 and was originally a coaching inn on the Ashbourne to Uttoxeter road.

It is a cosy little place with a main bar and dining areas.

room. There is also en suite overnight accommodation. Food is available every day and among the starters on the varied menu are prawn cocktail, garlic mushrooms and home-made soup. Main courses include smoked salmon salad, fresh salmon steak, grilled lamb chops, rump steak, gammon steak, honey-glazed chicken fillet, rump of wild venison in port and red wine, roast beef, home-made steak and mushroom pie, Whitby scampi, ham, egg and chips and giant Yorkshire puddings filled with beef stew. There is also a traditional Sunday roast, a selection of home-made sweets, a specials board and a children's menu. Large parties are advised to book, especially at weekends. Bass and Theakston are available on draught. You will also find M&B Mild, Carling Black Label and Guinness. Outside is a play area for children and a garden, which overlooks Calwich Abbey. No dogs please.
    Telephone: 01335 324242.

How to get there: Ellastone lies midway between Uttoxeter and Ashbourne. From Uttoxeter follow the B5030 northwards. Join the B5032 and soon you reach the village of Ellastone. The inn is on the right, just beyond the B5033.

Parking: There is a small car park at the pub.

Length of the walk: 3¾ miles. Map: OS Landranger 119 Buxton, Matlock and Dove Dale area (GR 117432).

This pretty walk makes for the grounds of Calwich Abbey before heading for rolling farmland to the north of it. The return leg of the route offers charming views of Ellastone and its church, set amid some of Staffordshire's most attractive countryside.

The Walk
Turn left on leaving the inn and walk along the B5032. Pass a telephone box, a row of bungalows and then houses. On the left is Bentley Fold Farm. Take the next turning on the left (Dove Street) and follow it for about ¼ mile. Pass an old water pump on the left. The lane runs between various stone cottages and houses. Pass Mill Lane and the post office and, as the road swings right, bear left by a stone lodge. Follow the drive between wrought iron and wooden fencing towards Calwich Abbey.

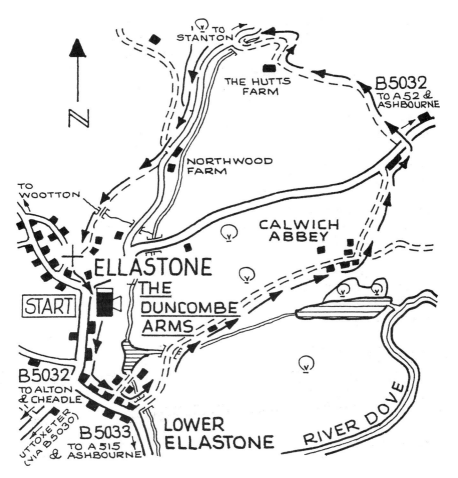

Cross a stream, then pass through a wooden gate with a sign – 'please keep dog on lead, sheep grazing'. The track curves to the right and cuts through this pleasant parkland. Over to the left are widespread views out towards the limestone summit of Weaver Hill and the village of Wootton sheltering in its shadow. Pass a cottage on the right, go through another gate and continue across the parkland. Beyond another gate you reach the remains of Calwich Abbey. The original abbey dates back to the Normans, when an Augustinian monastery was established here on the pretty banks of the Dove. The monks were routed in 1530 and the abbey was subsequently converted into a private house, which was eventually demolished. Handel was a frequent visitor to Calwich, and is reputed to have composed the *Messiah* here.

Pass a collection of dilapidated farm buildings and continue as far as a bungalow. Turn left at this point and follow the drive round to the right of a house. Beyond the next gate follow the track across the fields to the road. Bear right, descend the slope and at the end of a row of houses on the right, turn left at a footpath sign for 'Stanton'. Cross the field to a gate and go straight ahead in the next field to another gate. Continue ahead towards a ruined barn and, as you draw level with it, begin to veer left to the field boundary where there is a basic stile. Ahead of you is a spectacular view across a richly wooded valley, with Stanton, Wootton and Weaver Hill in the distance.

Drop down the slope towards the farm buildings. Aim a little to the right of them, to reach a white gate. Follow the track as it zig-zags down through several more gates and then swing right just before the farmyard. Follow the main farm track away from the buildings and down towards the road. After several minutes you come to a stile on the right. Cross it and descend the steep, grassy slope to a little footbridge. Cross the stream, swing half-left and then you come to the road on a bend.

Continue ahead, pass the farm entrance and follow the lane alongside the stream. Continue beyond Northwood Farm and a cluster of cottages and after about 70 yards you will see a stile in the right-hand bank. Look for Ellastone church tower in the distance and head towards it. Cross the field diagonally to a stile on the far side. Go through a little copse and in the subsequent field continue ahead to the next boundary. Pass over a stream and then make for the stile in the top boundary.

Follow the left edge of the next field towards the church. Cross the next stile by an oak tree and then veer right to the gate into Ellastone churchyard. Turn left and walk along its edge. Pass various yew trees and go down to the lychgate. The church tower was built in 1586, the chancel two years later in 1588 – the year of the Armada. Much of the church was rebuilt in the 19th century.

Go out to the road, turn left and then at the junction bear left again. At the junction with the B5032 turn right and the inn is on the left.

22 Alton
The Bull's Head Inn

Alton, situated in the glorious Churnet valley, is probably most closely associated with the famous theme park of Alton Towers. The village has a long history, which can be traced back to Saxon times, and is mentioned in the Domesday Book. Originally it was known as Alverton.

The Bull's Head, located in the main street, is one of several pubs in Alton. In summer this locally famous 18th century inn and hotel can get very busy when tourists and day trippers crowd into the village in search of refreshment. Inside, there is a pleasant old, beamed bar, with various horse brasses, exposed stone walls, a quaint inglenook fireplace and alcoves. Note the jugs hanging from the ceiling, as well as an old bayonet and military rifle, and an aerial view of the pub. In addition to the bar there is a restaurant and function room. The Bull's Head also offers bed and breakfast accommodation and there is a snug off the bar area. Bass and Marston's Pedigree feature among the beers, and you will also find

Carling, Stella and Dry Blackthorn cider. There is Guinness too. Dishes include pâté, soup, toasted sandwiches, steak and ale pudding, chicken and broccoli bake, moussaka and Italian meat balls. There is a daily specials board, too. Children are permitted in the restaurant, for which it is advisable to book. The menu is more limited out of season, so it is best to check the availability of food by telephone.
Telephone: 01538 702307.

How to get there: Alton lies south-east of Stoke-on-Trent. From the A522, which runs from Uttoxeter to join the A52, take the B5032 eastwards from Cheadle. The Bull's Head is in Alton's High Street, near the church.

Parking: There is room to park at the Bull's Head. Alton also has some parking spaces.

Length of the walk: 4 miles. Map: OS Landranger 119 Buxton, Matlock and Dove Dale area (GR 073423).

Many hidden delights await you in the gloriously wooded Churnet valley, aptly dubbed the 'Staffordshire Rhineland', most of which are reserved only for those who visit this delightful area on foot. The route I have chosen is a popular, well-trodden one but, as a walk, it is hard to equal. From Alton you head west through the valley to Dimmings Dale. The youth hostel here represents the halfway point of the walk. The thickly wooded return leg to Alton is no less pretty.

The Walk
Turn left from the front door of the inn and then right at the junction. Pass Alton Methodist church and the Wild Duck Inn. Follow the road round several bends and at the bottom of the hill, just before the Churnet, turn left by the entrance to the Bridge House Hotel. When the lane bears left by some cottages, go straight on, passing the National Trust sign for 'Toothill Wood' on the left. This is a pretty spot – the Churnet winding through the meadows and pastures to the right of you, woodland climbing the bank to your left.
Follow the lane round several sharp bends and then take the

track signposted to 'Smelting Mill and Dimmings Dale'. The track passes to the left of a stone cottage and continues through the woodland. The river is visible between the trees, far below you on the right. The outline of the Rambler's Retreat can also be spotted down in the valley. This inn and restaurant, with its garden and summertime parasols, is featured on the return leg of the walk.

At a fork, veer left and continue on a grassy path, with stone cottages on the right. Aim for a gate and a squeeze stile. Follow the grassy path across the field. On the left are sandstone cliffs. Pass a gate into a field on the right and continue on the muddy path through the gorse bushes. Head for a stile ahead of you, on the edge of thick woodland. Follow the path down through the trees and, at the bottom of the bank, go down some steps to a forest track.

Turn left and pass between the trees. At the time this book was written, there was a wreath pinned to the bark of a tree on this stretch of the walk. The inscription on the card read, 'RSM Tom Beardmore, Number 9 Commando Unit, killed in action at Anzio, February 2nd or 3rd 1943. He loved this place but like so many others, he didn't make it home. Always remembered. The Family'. A touching tribute to a casualty of war.

Further along, on the left, is a path to the Peakstone Inn. Carry on past a turning to Gentleman's Rock and, a couple of steps beyond it, turn right, passing a pond and the lip of a weir. Aim for the steep path ahead of you, climbing between the trees. At the top of the bank you reach a junction of paths. Turn left and go on up through the woodland. Follow the track as it curves round to the right. Keep going as it climbs steeply between lines of trees. Soon you will see a path running off to the left to a seat by a huge sandstone crag. There is a marvellous view from here back across the Churnet valley.

Take the path and, after several yards, you come to a gate and a sign for 'The Ranger'. This is a Site of Special Scientific Interest. Now in the care of Forest Enterprise, it is one of Staffordshire's most important remaining ancient hill pastures. The field is being grazed by livestock to help promote wild flowers. Near the gate is a plaque to the memory of Paul Rey, a rambler and world traveller who inspired so many with his love of the countryside.

Follow the well-trodden path between gorse bushes, keeping the stone wall on your left. At the next gate is a sign for Dimmings

Dale Youth Hostel. Follow the path alongside the buildings of the hostel and then head down the track away from them. Soon you reach a sign on the right for the Staffordshire Way. Join the route and after a few moments you reach a junction of three paths. Take the path on the left and follow it through the mixed woodland of Ousal Dale.

The path, wide and muddy in places, descends at a pleasantly gentle pace between banks of bracken and lines of larch trees. Note the lichen growing in profusion on the rocky outcrops. Some of the rock formations on this stretch of the walk have been sculptured into fascinating shapes. One giant slab of sandstone rears up beside you like the awesome hull of a giant ocean-going liner. Follow the path as it swings sharply right and then bears left. Join a wide track running alongside the large fish pond. There was once a smelting mill here. By the late 18th century it had become a corn grinding mill where a water wheel drove three pairs of stones.

Follow the track to the Rambler's Retreat and then continue along the road towards Alton. There are fascinating glimpses of Alton Castle from here. In a certain light, with its dark, Gothic design and rocky position high above the gorge, it has the romantic fairytale appeal of a Rhineland castle.

Return to the Bridge House Hotel, then bear right and pass to the left of the Talbot Inn. Follow the stepped path and, further up, you join the road. From here it is only a short walk back to the pub in the centre of Alton. If time allows, you can take a stroll around the village streets where there is much to see. Look out for the distinctive, dome-shaped lock-up further up the hill. On the far side of the Churnet is Alton Towers, Britain's most popular leisure attraction.

23 Saverley Green
The Greyhound

Saverley Green is a pleasantly rural community on the river Blithe, a few miles from the sprawling suburbs of Stoke-on-Trent. The Greyhound is a picturesque, timber-framed inn, thought to have been built as a pub about 200 years ago. It has been largely extended over the years and now includes a bar lounge and a separate restaurant with a no smoking area. It is a popular locals' pub with plenty of character.

There is an extensive choice of food. The bar menu includes various sandwiches and jacket potatoes, as well as soup, pâté, toast and salad, cod or haddock and chips, lasagne, beef and Guinness pie, chilli con carne, beef curry and rice, chicken and scampi. Salads and ploughman's lunches are also available, as are children's meals – among them fish fingers, sausages or chicken nuggets and chips. The à la carte menu lists various starters, fish dishes, steaks, grills, chicken and game, chef's specialities and vegetarian choices. A traditional Sunday roast is served and you will find a daily specials board, giving even more choice. The

restaurant is not open on Monday. You are advised to book at weekends. Among the real ales to be found at the inn are Bass and Worthington Bitter. There is usually a guest ale as well. Carling, Grolsch, Kronenbourg, M&B Mild and Scrumpy Jack cider are also available. There is also a children's play area and a pets' corner. Dogs are not permitted inside.
Telephone: 01782 395576.

How to get there: Saverley Green is just south of the A50 between Stoke-on-Trent and Uttoxeter. Turn off at Cresswell towards Fulford. Cross the railway line, then bear right at an inn, the Hunter. Go through Saverley Green and the pub is on the right at the end of the village.

Parking: There is a spacious car park at the side of the inn.

Length of the walk: 3½ miles. Map: OS Landranger 127 Stafford, Telford and surrounding area (GR 965385).

This is a very pleasant country walk crossing a peaceful tract of countryside between the rivers Trent and Blithe. Midway round the route is the pretty village of Fulford.

The Walk
From the inn turn right for a few steps, then bear left over a stile in the hedgerow. Walk ahead, keeping a line of trees and holly bushes on the left. Aim for the bottom left-hand corner of the field, then cross two stiles with a footbridge in between. Continue straight ahead to another footbridge. Go ahead for several yards towards some holly trees and bear left over another footbridge into the adjacent field. Turn right, cross another footbridge, then aim for the rim of a wooded hollow. Head for the road and turn right.

Pass the entrances to New House Farm and The Limes. This stretch of the walk provides good views over rolling farmland and woodland. Just beyond the entrance to The Hollies, look for a stile and gate on the right. Cross the field diagonally to the bottom left-hand corner. Go into the next field, then bear immediately left at a stile. Turn right and follow the field edge.

Make for the field corner, cross the stile and continue ahead, with the hedge line on the right. Cross a stile in the corner and in

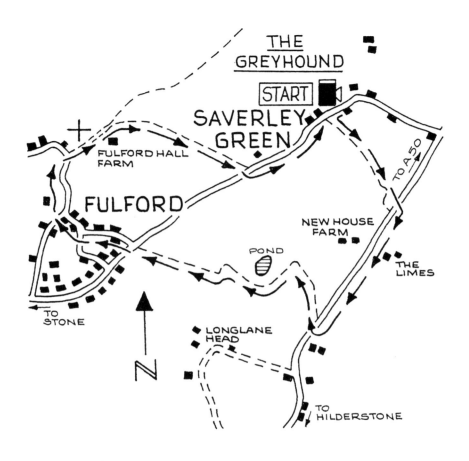

front of you is a pond. Follow the path to the left of it, keeping on the higher ground above the water. Cross the next stile, turn right and walk along the field boundary. In the corner, join a path enclosed by wire fencing and trees. Continue for a few yards to a stile. Just beyond it swing right and follow a line of bushes on the right, as you progress down the field. Cross a marshy ditch and then head for a line of trees. Beyond them you head up the field slope to the far boundary. Look for a stile in the hedgerow. Descend the steps to the road and cross over into Meadow Lane, lined by neo-Georgian houses.

Soon you pass the Shoulder of Mutton inn on the right. Walk ahead alongside Fulford's pretty village green. Follow the lane as it curves to the right and heads for St Nicholas's church, prominently located away from the centre of Fulford. There has been a place of worship on this site since the 14th century, and in the early 19th century the church was a popular choice with eloping couples anxious to get married.

Follow the track, sometimes muddy, beyond the church and between farm buildings. Further on, the track reaches some gates. Continue on between holly trees to a stile. This sheltered bridleway, cutting through a tunnel of trees, is one of the highlights of this walk. In places the little-used route can be somewhat overgrown. Cross another stile and at the road turn left. Follow the road back to the inn.

24 Salt
The Holly Bush Inn

The village of Salt probably takes its name from the salt marshes to be found in the area. Situated on the banks of the Trent – on rising ground to prevent flooding – it is a pretty place, thankfully removed from the march of traffic on the A51 about ½ mile away.

The thatched Holly Bush Inn is reputedly the second oldest fully licensed inn in the country. Dating back over 800 years, the building was once a baiting house for ponies, asses and mules carrying salt from nearby Shirleywich to Stafford and beyond. According to a newspaper cutting, dated 1938, the inn is 'steeped in history, with a thousand tales to tell' and 'at the rear of the house there were stables and a blacksmith's shop, which suggested that the Holly Bush may once have been used as a coaching house, though, of course, it was not on any of the old routes.' Part of the kitchen was destroyed in a fire in the 1920s, the fire brigade's arrival being delayed by fog.

Inside, there are low beams, much exposed brick and stone and a cosy fire. Bass is among the real ales, while lagers include Stella

Artois, Labatts and Carling Black Label. You will also find Guinness, Murphys and Scrumpy Jack cider. The Holly Bush is open all day Saturday and Sunday for food and drink. Food is available every day and among the varied dishes usually available are mixed grill, breaded scampi, whole braised ham hock, rabbit casserole and chargrilled red sea bream. There are also sandwiches and ploughman's lunches. There are various children's meals and a range of daily specials. On Sunday a traditional roast is served. No dogs please.

Telephone: 01889 508234.

How to get there: Salt is close to the A51, between Stone and Rugeley, and is near its junction with the A518 Stafford road at Weston. On leaving the A51 cross the Trent, turn right at the junction and the inn is on the left.

Parking: The Holly Bush has its own car park. Please consult the landlord if leaving a vehicle here while doing the walk.

Length of the walk: 3¼ miles. Map: OS Landranger 127 Stafford, Telford and surrounding area (GR 957277).

This is a delightful walk in the Trent valley. From Salt the route heads for the wooded slopes, before passing close to the site of the Civil War battle of Hopton Heath. The walk returns to the valley floor via several peaceful paths, tracks and stretches of road.

The Walk
From the inn bear left and walk along Salt's main street. At a telephone box turn left to join a public footpath cutting between houses. Just beyond them you reach a junction of paths. Avoid the path on the left and go forward to a stile and gate. In the next field head for the hillside and line of trees on the horizon. After about 70 yards, at the hedge corner, veer left and go up the slope, with the boundary fence on the left.

On reaching the higher ground keep to the edge of a burst of woodland, so that the trees are on your immediate right. Make for the field corner, cross three siles in quick succession and walk ahead across a pasture. Keep to the left of several cottages, cross a stile and then veer a little to the right, down to a stile by some trees.

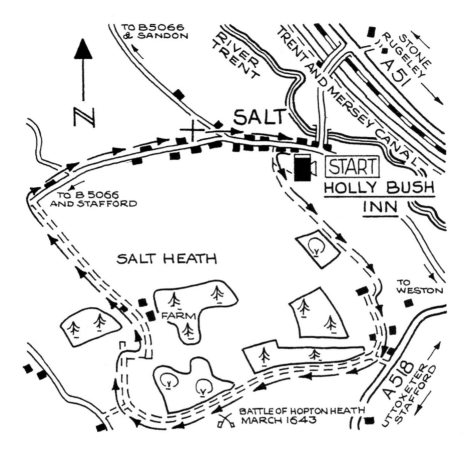

Turn left and follow the tarmac drive. Soon the drive becomes
stony and cuts between various groups of cottages. At the
junction, with the A518 a short distance to the left, bear right
and follow a track. Note the bridleway sign here. Pass alongside
belts of pretty woodland and further on you reach a smallholding
or homestead. Continue on the bridleway, pass a track on the right
and walk on beside lines of trees.

To the south lies Hopton Heath where, in March 1643,
Parliamentary and Royalist forces clashed, with bloody con-
sequences. It was the biggest Civil War battle ever to take place
in the county. The Earl of Northampton, who led the Royalists,

became a casualty of the conflict when his horse was shot and he was subsequently engulfed by enemy soldiers. He stubbornly refused to surrender right up to the end. Relics from the battle, including a rusty scimitar about 20 inches long, have been found at the Holly Bush Inn.

Pass a 'private woodland' sign and continue. Beyond the trees the track, muddy in places, cuts between fields, trees and hedgerows. At the next junction turn right and follow the track between hedges until you reach a sign 'private woodland – no access'. Turn right here and cross a stile. Go straight across the field to a stile beside a gate. Cross it and follow the track north under the branches of various oak trees. Pass several houses and farm buildings and continue to the road. Turn right and follow the lane back to Salt.

Beyond the village sign you cut between houses and cottages of quite distinctive architecture. Pass the village church of St James the Great. This is mid-19th century and was built, in Gothic style, with stones from nearby Weston Quarry. A plaque at the entrance states that the churchyard gates were dedicated on Easter Day 1968 'in loving memory of Mr and Mrs Samuel Holford and family of Weston Quarry, who were faithful members of this church for many years.' Continue through the village, pass the telephone box encountered earlier and return to the inn.

25 Abbots Bromley
The Coach and Horses

Abbots Bromley is one of Staffordshire's most famous villages. There are many old and historic buildings of note, and at one time the village boasted as many as 15 public houses.

The Coach and Horses was one of that number and, thankfully, it still survives today. It was first licensed in 1745 and became a coaching inn on the Midland and North-East route. Several sources indicate that it was once a correction house for wayward monks, some being reputed to have been walled up in the pub's cellar. Even today there are stories which suggest that this part of the inn is haunted by the imprisoned brothers. The inn comprises a main bar, dining area and garden room. There are a number of charming features, including beams, jugs, tankards and horse brasses. Outside is a pretty beer garden and terrace and a play area for children. Bed and breakfast accommodation is also provided.

Food is available every day and among the bar snacks are chilli con carne, beef curry, cod in beer batter, various omelettes, ploughman's lunches, filled jacket potatoes, beef lasagne, cottage pie and lamb chops, together with sandwiches and rolls. The dining room menu lists starters, steaks, fish dishes, salads and vegetarian choices. There is also a range of sweets, a children's menu, a traditional Sunday lunch and a specials board.

Beers on handpump include Tetley Bitter, Bass and Marston's Pedigree. Worthington Best Bitter is on keg, and the lager drinker will find Carling Black Label, Carlsberg and Stella Artois. Telephone: 01283 840256.

How to get there: From Uttoxeter follow the B5013, then the B5014 eastwards to Abbots Bromley. The inn is on the left beyond the village centre. From Lichfield follow the A515, then the B5014 northwards to Abbots Bromley. The inn is on the right.

Parking: There is a car park at the rear of the pub. Otherwise park in Abbots Bromley, where there are usually spaces.

Length of the walk: 2¾ miles. Map: OS Landranger 128 Derby and Burton-upon-Trent area (GR 084244).

This walk begins by exploring the village of Abbots Bromley, part of the Needwood Forest. Beyond the village the route follows a stretch of the Staffordshire Way where there are glimpses of the smooth expanse of Blithfield Reservoir in the distance. The walk returns to Abbots Bromley along pleasant field paths.

The Walk

From the pub turn right and walk along the main street of the village. Pass the school of St Mary and St Anne on the right and continue between lines of houses and cottages. Pass the post office and veer left by the war memorial. Note the picturesque timber-framed Goat's Head Inn nearby.

The butter cross in the centre of the village would have been the focal point of Abbots Bromley in the days when it was a bustling market town. Mary Queen of Scots spent a night here in 1586 and then again as she journeyed to Fotheringay Castle where she was executed in 1587. There are several local legends and customs associated with Abbots Bromley. Probably the most famous of these is the annual September Horn Dance, believed to have religious or possibly ritualistic connections. It may originally

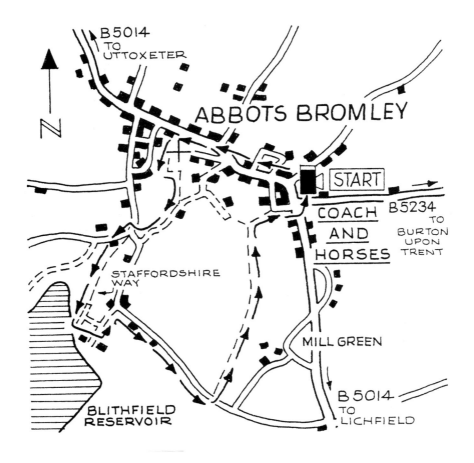

have been some kind of fertility dance or a celebration of hunting rights in the Forest of Needwood. On the first Monday after 4th September six men wearing reindeer antlers gather in the village centre. With them are two musicians on accordion and triangle, a man on a hobby horse, a jester, a maid and a boy with a bow and arrow. The horns were carbon-dated in the late 1970s and evidence indicates they date from the second half of the 11th century. The horns are kept in the parish church.

Follow the lane to the left of the butter cross and go along to the churchyard. Cross it diagonally to the far corner. Take the path over the swirling stream, and follow it for about 50 yards.

Look for a stile in the left boundary. Cross the field and on the left is a good view of the church. When the power cables swing right continue ahead, with the stream parallel to you on the left. At the far end of the meadow cross the stream, via the footbridge and make for the next stile.

Turn right and follow the green lane. Very soon the track switches to a concrete surface. Pass the entrance to the sewage treatment works and continue to the point where the track veers right at a cattle grid. Go straight on through a gate and along the field boundary to a lane. Bear right and walk along to the next junction. Turn left at a stile and follow the route of the Staffordshire Way. Make for the gap in the next hedgerow.

Cross the stile and ahead of you Blithfield Reservoir gradually edges into view. The reservoir, part of Blithfield Park, was officially opened in 1953 and supplies water to a population of $1\frac{1}{4}$ million in an area of almost 600 square miles. The shoreline and surrounding woodlands of oak, sycamore and beech include a wide variety of plants – marsh marigold, primrose and bluebell among them. The reservoir, an important habitat for many types of birds, is also a popular recreational area. Sailing is the main leisure pursuit here. Over to the right, in the far distance, you can see the façade of Blithfield Hall.

Aim for the next boundary, cross the stile and continue alongside a line of trees. In the field corner walk ahead along a path lined with trees and banks of vegetation. At the next stile bear left to join a muddy track. Follow it to a drive and at this point you part company with the Staffordshire Way. Turn left and head towards some houses. On reaching the road at a bend, bear right. Follow the lane past the farm and take the next stile on the left (signposted 'Abbots Bromley'). Pass under the power lines and begin to head diagonally across the field to the far left corner. Drop down the bank to a stile and footbridge. Follow the field edge and the next stile is hidden in the hedgerow in the corner. Cross the stile, go straight on for several yards and then turn left. Follow the field boundary and in the corner go straight on along a narrow path.

The school buildings of St Mary and St Anne can be seen now. Do not cross the next stile but bear right immediately before it and follow the path across the playing fields. Beyond them, join a lane down to the road and turn left. The inn is on the right.

Tutbury

Ye Olde Dog and Partridge

Tutbury is steeped in history. One of its chief attractions is the old ruined castle. Ye Olde Dog and Partridge, with its half-timbered frontage, is surely one of the most picturesque buildings in the little town. The interior is heavily beamed and the walls are covered with various black and white photographs and prints of local hunting scenes. This coaching inn dates back to the 15th century and was extended in the 18th and 19th centuries. For some years it was closely associated with the tradition of bull running, originating at the time of John of Gaunt. A mutilated bull was released by the townspeople of Tutbury. If caught before sunset, they could claim it; if not, the animal remained the property of the prior. The bull was subsequently attached to a bull ring nearby and baited with dogs. No doubt this practice would have proved to be very popular with today's animal rights protestors!

The Carvery Restaurant is open for lunch and dinner seven days a week. The carvery buffet has achieved national acclaim with its freshly cooked meats, traditional roast beef, fresh seafood and a

dessert buffet that is second to none. In addition, the Brasserie Restaurant offers a vibrant, informal atmosphere where you can enjoy high quality fresh local produce imaginatively presented with a modern flair. For something more modest, try the Brasserie Bar where there is a varied choice of open sandwiches, baguettes, cold meats and starters. The bar serves Marston's Pedigree, Stella Artois, Heineken and a different guest beer every month. Large groups are advised to book and children are welcome. With its comfortable accommodation, the hotel is an ideal base for a walking weekend in the area.
  Telephone: 01283 813030.

How to get there: Tutbury is north of Burton-upon-Trent, on the A50. From Uttoxeter follow the A50 towards Burton. The hotel is in the High Street.

Parking: There is a car park at the rear of Ye Olde Dog and Partridge. If you prefer, you could use the car park in Duke Street.

Length of the walk: 2¾ miles. Map: OS Landranger 128 Derby and Burton-upon-Trent area (GR 214288).

From the town and its main street of Tudor, Georgian and Regency buildings, the walk heads for the site of the romantic castle ruins and then leaves Tutbury altogether to follow the banks of the pretty river Dove. The return leg of the route is dominated by views of the castle across the fields.

The Walk
From the front door of Ye Olde Dog and Partridge turn left, then bear right into Duke Street. Pass the Leopard Inn and continue up the slope to the entrance to Tutbury Castle. On the right here is the Norman church of St Mary the Virgin. In the churchyard you will see the imposing monument 'in memory of Henry Edwards Esq who practised as a surgeon in this town for 45 years and served in a similar capacity in the 43rd Regiment during the Peninsula War. He died on 11th day of November 1863 aged 74. This monument was erected by his friends as a tribute of their regard and esteem.'
  The castle occupies a commanding position on an isolated rock

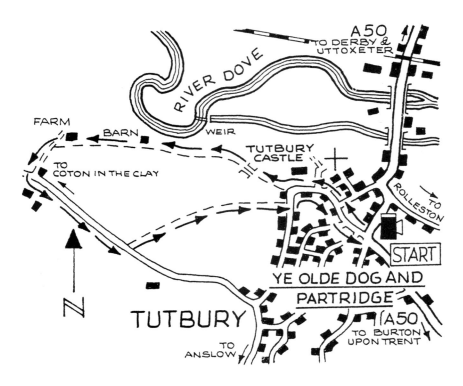

overlooking the surrounding area. Long before it was built, there was an Iron Age fort here. Like so many other ruined strongholds in this area, Tutbury Castle was besieged by Parliamentary forces. However, the remains of John of Gaunt's gateway are still visible, as is the high tower where Mary Queen of Scots was held in captivity. The castle is open to the public between Easter and the end of September.

Retrace your steps to the road and bear right. As the road bends left, signposted 'Park Lane', swing right to join a public footpath. Ahead of you is a glorious panorama – the river Dove meandering through the countryside with thousands of acres of Derbyshire farmland on the far side of it.

Descend the stepped path to the corner of the field. Head towards the river Dove and behind you Tutbury Castle rises skyward. Pass through a gap into the adjoining field and after several yards, bear left over a stile. Follow the path's vague

110

outline diagonally across the field. Make for the boundary, cross a footbridge and then veer half-left towards a stile. Just before reaching it, swing sharp right and follow the path directly to the Dove river bank. A few steps along the bank brings you to a weir where the scene is very pretty.

Retrace your steps along the river bank, keeping to the path nearest the river. Cross a stile and pass some dilapidated barns and brick sheds. The Dove begins to snake away to the right at this point. Continue ahead across the field to a gate in the next boundary. Cross the field to the left-hand corner, pass into the next field and continue along the boundary to a white gate by a cottage. Go out to the road and turn left. Follow the straight road until just before it begins to curve left. There is a farm up on the hill ahead. Cross the stile in the left-hand hedgerow and veer half-right towards the outline of Tutbury Castle. Cross a grassy mound to reach the bottom of the field, where there is a stile. In the next field go straight ahead on a muddy track. After about 150 yards veer right to cross two stiles in the boundary. Then bear right and head up the right-hand edge of the field to a stile. Join a concrete lane and walk up to the road. Bear left and return to the centre of Tutbury.

27 Milford
The Barley Mow

Milford is a pleasant village, with a spacious, grassy common, on the A513 Stafford to Lichfield road. Close by is the National Trust's Shugborough Estate, which is open to visitors.

The Barley Mow is a large, rambling old inn on the main road. It is a favourite watering hole of walkers heading for Cannock Chase, and visitors to Shugborough Hall. Inside are various alcoves and the decor has a strong Victorian theme to it. Apart from the roomy bar, there is also a restaurant.

Beer drinkers can choose from several ales on handpump, including Tetley Bitter and Bass available on keg and you will also find Guinness, Carlsberg, Grolsh and Carling Black Label. For the cider drinker there is Dry Blackthorn on draught. Food is available every day, and all day on Sunday. Bar snacks include soup, filled jacket potatoes, with cheese and bacon and tuna and mayonnaise among the flavours, grilled burgers, hot and cold filled baguettes – including bacon, sausage and onion, 5 oz rump steak and cheese, coleslaw and pickle – and a variety of

cold platters. Hot main dishes range from steak and kidney pie and lasagne verdi to scampi and fried haddock. Large groups are requested to book for bar snacks. The restaurant, for which it is also advisable to book, offers a selection of starters, various steaks, grills and home-made specials. Vegetarians are catered for, too. A specials board lists further choices, and a Sunday carvery and daily breakfast are available. Children are welcome; no dogs please. The inn is open all day in summer.
Telephone: 01785 661079.

How to get there: Milford's main road is part of the A513 between Stafford and Rugeley. The inn is on the north side of the road, at the eastern end of the village.

Parking: There is a spacious car park at the pub. Alternatively, you could park on Milford Common which is opposite the Barley Mow.

Length of the walk: 3¾ miles. Map: OS Landranger 127 Stafford, Telford and surrounding area (GR 973213).

Apart from the many and varied attractions offered by this walk, there is also a short, optional detour to Shugborough Hall, the splendid 900-acre ancestral home of the Earls of Lichfield. The main route of the walk follows a series of delightful woodland paths and tracks taking you deep into the heart of Cannock Chase.

The Walk

On leaving the pub bear left and pass Bostons Fiat Garage, then follow the residential road running parallel to the main A513. Pass The Red House and Rose Cottage and, at the junction, turn right. Walk beside lines of beech trees and, at the next junction, you will see the entrance to Shugborough Hall on the left. Among the estate's attractions are a country museum and farmstead, various monuments and acres of sprawling parkland. Dating back to the late 17th century, the house has seen many changes over the years. The eight distinctive Ionic columns, which form the grand portico, were added by Samuel Wyatt, the famous architect. Today, Shugborough Hall is the home of Patrick Lichfield, the distinguished photographer and second cousin to Her Majesty the Queen.

From the main gate of Shugborough Hall go straight across the road and then veer slightly right between some beech trees to join a clear path. There are good views on the right down to Milford Common and the houses overlooking it. Follow the path between bracken, gorse bushes and lines of oak trees. Soon the sound of traffic on the main road recedes as you plunge deeper into the woodland.

Cannock Chase was once a royal forest where Plantagenet kings hunted game. Its exclusive royal status may have gone but, within its 26 square miles, Cannock Chase has much to offer the visitor. It is administered by Forest Enterprise and there are picnic sites, pools, great heather expanses and pleasant woodland rides to enjoy. There may also be the rare glimpse of a fallow deer to savour, and the chance to stumble upon glacial remnants from the Ice Age, in the shape of great granite boulders and rocks dotted about the landscape. On the higher ground you will see Anson's Pines. These trees were planted late in the 18th century to mark the voyage of Admiral Anson, First Lord of the Admiralty, round the world in 1740. Anson's brother lived at Shugborough Hall.

Descend the slope towards a pond and then veer a little to the left of it, avoiding the clear track on the left. Follow the stepped path and from the crest of the hill there are very good views of Milford, with the buildings of Stafford in the distance and, nearer to hand, the bracken-covered mounds of Cannock Chase. Drop down the slope to a stony track and continue through the trees until you reach a junction of parallel paths. Take the second path from the right, noting an iron bar or rail beside the route. Follow the path between trees and bracken. At the next junction continue ahead towards Coppice Hill. There is a pool on the right, amidst the trees. The path curves gradually to the right and begins to climb. On the right are glimpses of the Wrekin on the Shropshire horizon. Eventually you reach a parking area.

Turn left at the junction (signposted 'stepping stones'). Follow the track alongside a coppice of larch trees. At the next junction bear right for a few steps, then follow the track as it curves left. An expansive area of Cannock Chase is visible at this point, giving the visitor some indication of the sheer size and scale of this wooded playground. During the First World War there was

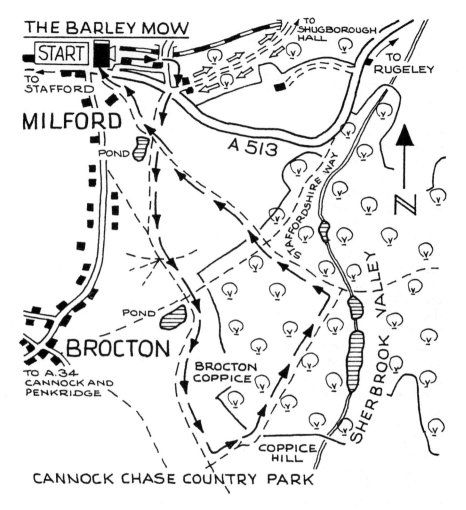

THE BARLEY MOW

START

TO STAFFORD

MILFORD

POND

A 513

TO SHUGBOROUGH HALL

TO RUGELEY

STAFFORDSHIRE WAY

N

POND

BROCTON

TO A.34 CANNOCK AND PENKRIDGE

BROCTON COPPICE

SHERBROOK VALLEY

COPPICE HILL

CANNOCK CHASE COUNTRY PARK

an army training camp based on Cannock Chase. Even today, many years on, there are still a few ghostly reminders of those days and the occasional concrete block or level grassy area can be seen. Follow the track between carpets of bracken and rows of birch trees.

Further on, the path drops down steeply into the delightful Sherbrook valley. As you approach the stepping stones over the stream, bear left and follow a clear path through the bracken. This is the route of the Staffordshire Way. At the next junction go straight on up the steep bank towards Milford. The views from the top are spectacular, as you look across a rolling, rumpled carpet of bracken to the vast urban landscape of Stafford and the Potteries beyond. Pass the pond skirted near the start of the walk and, with the water on your left, make for the wooden barrier and swing right to the parking area. Pass the Sister Dora home for the elderly and, as the track swings left, continue on a path down to Milford Common. The inn is visible on the far side.

28 Cannock Wood
The Park Gate Inn

Cannock Wood is one of a chain of communities strung out along the southern boundary of Cannock Chase. This small collection of houses and cottages, overlooking the countryside of mid-Staffordshire, represents the highest point on Cannock Chase.

Originally part of the Marquis of Anglesey's estate, the inn, which dates back to about 1640, was once the venue for many grand, stately banquets. The pub's restaurant used to be where local tenants came to pay their rent to the landowner. The Park Gate Bar is now the Ramblers Bar – there are lots of paintings, solid beams, panelled alcoves and horse brasses. A delightful old brick and beamed fireplace, with a warming woodburning stove glowing in winter, adds to the cosiness of the room.

There is an extensive choice of main meals including pork and apple pie, cod in batter, fisherman's pie, sweet and sour duck, mixed grill, traditional fish and chips, steak and kidney pie, half a roast chicken and cod in prawn bake. There are also Chinese and Louisiana sizzlers, various baguettes, hot sandwiches, club sandwiches and all-day breakfasts. A specials board lists further choices and there is a traditional Sunday roast. The restaurant menu has a number of starters, including pâté, breaded mushrooms, potato skins and smoked mackerel. It is advisable to book. On handpump are several real ales, including Marston's Pedigree, Ansells Bitter and Greene King IPA. Stella Artois, Fosters, Carlsberg, Guinness, and Scrumpy Jack and Strongbow cider are also on offer. The bar is open all day. Children are welcome in the lounge and restaurant. Outside is a beer garden and a play area.

Telephone: 01543 682223.

How to get there: Follow the A5190 between Lichfield and Cannock. At the junction with the B5011 Brownhills road head north towards Gentleshaw and Cannock Wood. After about 2 miles you reach a junction. Go straight over into Bradwell Lane. At the next junction turn left (signposted Castle Ring) and the inn is on the right. There are other roads in the area signposted to Castle Ring. Follow any of them and you will find the inn opposite the car park.

Parking: There is a car park at the inn. If it is busy you could park across the road at Castle Ring.

Length of the walk: 2¾ miles. Map: OS Landranger 128 Derby and Burton-upon-Trent area (GR 046125).

Castle Ring is one of Cannock Chase's most famous landmarks. The walk skirts the fort to head north and then east across the Chase before returning to Castle Ring. At times there are stunning views of the sprawling woodland and forest.

The Walk

From the inn turn right and, at the junction, go straight across into the car park at Castle Ring. This is the largest of the seven Iron Age forts in Staffordshire. It was built between 500 BC

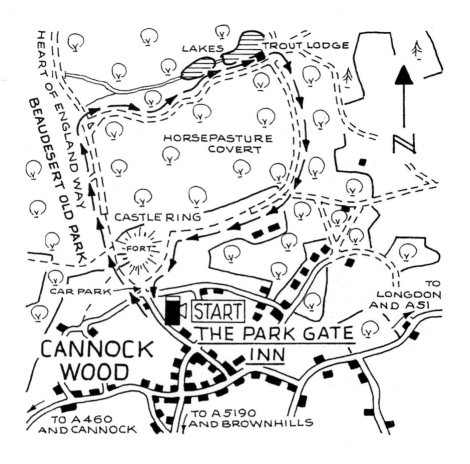

and AD 43 and covers about 9 acres. At almost 800 ft above sea level, it is the highest point on the Chase. Before the surrounding trees were planted, there would have been magnificent views in all directions, and the fort would certainly have protected the local farming community from the threat of invaders. Evidence suggests that it may have been occupied until about AD 500. It later became the site of what is thought to be a medieval hunting lodge in the days when Cannock Chase was a royal forest, comprising dense oak woodland. Today, many of the trees are gone but Cannock Chase survives as a popular amenity area on the doorstep of the industrial and urban West Midlands.

At the far end of the car park, where the paths fork, take the left-hand branch, following the waymarker post. Pass over a track and continue. On the right are glimpses of the power station near Rugeley. Soon you come down to a track. Turn right and head north towards the plantations of Beaudesert Old Park, once the estate of the Marquis of Anglesey. You may see thinning being carried out. The trees that are cut down ultimately end up as paper, fencing or other wood products.

At the next junction, where a track sweeps in from the left, continue ahead. Go down to a triangular junction and bear right. Follow the track, passing lines of larch trees, carpets of bracken and pretty woodland glades. At the next junction, where you can see the outline of a lake and, on its shore, a chalet, Trout Lodge, through the trees on the left, turn sharp right and follow the track up the gradual slope. Further up, there are far-reaching views back across Cannock Chase.

Soon the track narrows and becomes quite muddy in places. Follow the path between beech trees and keep to it as it curves to the right. Pass over a stream and then the path bears left to a fence. Turn right and follow the path, keeping the fence on your left. At the fence corner you reach another junction of paths. Turn left here. Houses are visible close by. After several steps swing right and make for a clear track. Turn left and follow the path along the perimeter of Castle Ring. After a few yards join the inner path and, when you reach some steps and railings, bear left and go down to the car park. Walk through it and return to the inn.

29 Fradley Junction
The Swan

Designated a conservation area and classed as a site of special architectural and historic interest, this is a bright and bustling sort of place – once, reputedly, the haunt of brandy smugglers, who no doubt used the conveniently located pub here. The Swan, which directly overlooks Fradley Junction, was built as an inn in 1780, three years after the completion of the Trent & Mersey Canal, generally regarded as Brindley's great engineering masterpiece. Today, this Grade II listed building is popular for its superb waterfront position, and in summer it can get very busy – the age of leisure and recreation and the revival of interest in our inland waterways bringing many new customers to the pub.

The interior of the Swan is cosy and full of character. It has a main bar, a lounge and an attractive cellar lounge, which was converted a few years ago from a warehousing and storage area. Note the low, vaulted brick ceiling. Food is served every day at the inn and the choice is varied. Examples of starters are prawn cocktail, seafood platter, soup and mushrooms in batter. Main

courses include mixed grill, T-bone steak, cottage pie, lasagne, steak and kidney pie, half a roast chicken and chicken Kiev. Breaded plaice, salmon with asparagus, cod, scampi, and seafood platter are among the fish dishes. There is a range of salads, including Bargee's Platter (prawn, ham, tuna, egg, cheese or beef), open sandwiches and bacon roll topped with grilled cheese. A children's menu is also available, as is a specials board at lunchtime and a traditional Sunday roast. As for drinks, you will find Strongbow draught cider, Stella and Carlsberg. Burton Ale, Ansells Mild and Bitter and Marston's Pedigree are all drawn on handpump. Well-behaved children and dogs are welcome. The Swan does not have a beer garden but there is room to sit at the front and watch the activity on the canal.
Telephone: 01283 790330.

How to get there: Take the A38 between Lichfield and Burton-upon-Trent. Follow the signs for Fradley village. Turn left in the village centre, pass the church and then continue to Fradley Junction. Cross the canal, then bear immediately left and drive along to the Swan.

Parking: There is a car park adjoining the inn. Please advise the landlord if leaving a vehicle here when the pub is closed.

Length of the walk: $3\frac{1}{4}$ miles. Map: OS Landranger 128 Derby and Burton-upon-Trent area (GR 141141).

There is always something to see at Fradley Junction, which is the meeting place of the Trent & Mersey and Coventry Canals. This pretty spot, with its moored narrow boats and charming old buildings, is a favourite haunt of the boating fraternity. The walk begins by following the towpath of the Coventry Canal. Beyond the village of Fradley, the route returns to Fradley Junction by crossing open farmland.

The Walk
Emerging from the inn onto the towpath of the Trent & Mersey Canal, turn left for a few yards towards Junction Lock, then cross the canal at the bridge. Bear right, pass Wharf House and follow the towpath of the Coventry Canal. This canal, linking Coventry

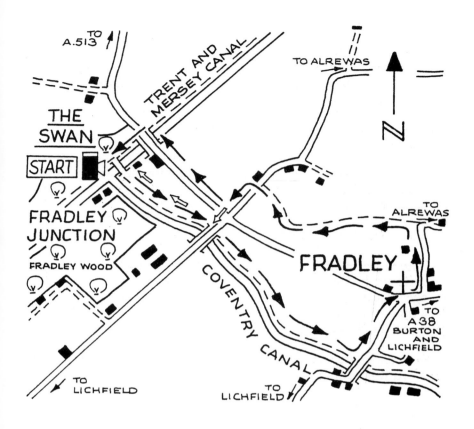

with the Trent & Mersey, was completed in 1790.

The canal curves a little to the left and on the right are the trees of Fradley Wood. Soon you reach the bridge at Gorse Lane. Continue, with views over wooded countryside. Immediately beyond the next bridge (number 90), go up the bank to the road and turn right towards Fradley village.

Bear right at the junction and pass the mid-19th century church of St Stephen, with its familiar yew trees. The church was built following an appeal from the vicar of neighbouring Alrewas, who insisted that the village should have its own place of worship. He also believed that it was too far to carry the departed to Alrewas for burial.

Immediately beyond the church turn left and follow the lane to the sharp right-hand bend. Make for the left of a bungalow, cross a dilapidated stile on the left and follow a track across the field. There is a hedge on the right. When you reach a fence in front of you, cross the stile and continue in the same direction, with the field boundary on your left (be prepared for some mud on this stretch of the walk).

As the boundary fence begins to curve left, in line with a stream, keep straight on and follow the track across the field. Make for the far boundary and as you approach it, swing right to follow the track along to the road. Turn left and follow the lane. Pass a pond on the left and soon you come to the junction.

At this point you have a choice of routes. Either return to Fradley Junction by turning right, following the road over the canal and then turning immediately left, or you can go straight across into Gorse Lane and retrace your steps along the towpath of the Coventry Canal. The inn soon comes into view at the junction of the two waterways.

③⓪ Harlaston
The White Lion

Harlaston is a pleasant conservation village on the banks of the Mease, one of Staffordshire's lesser-known rivers. The existence of a corn mill here merited the settlement a mention in the Domesday Book.

The White Lion, which is closed Monday lunchtime, is a striking pub, with a distinctive whitened façade. The building lies at the centre of a road junction, so that roads radiate from it in different directions. Originally much smaller, with an adjoining cottage, the inn has been extended and converted over the years. Parts of it are about 300 years old. The White Lion, allegedly, boasts spirits of the supernatural kind, as well as those you may find on offer in the bar! The ghost of a man has been seen on a number of occasions – thought to be that of a cavalier at the battle of Bosworth, which ended the Wars of the Roses in August 1485, a few miles to the east.

Food is served every day and, apart from the daily specials, there is a printed menu which lists various starters – home-made soup, prawn cocktail and pâté among them. The main courses include a

range of rump and T-bone steaks, deep-fried plaice filled with prawns and mushrooms, scampi, fresh fish, half a chargrilled chicken, breaded chicken breast, home-made steak and kidney pie, garlic and Cajun chicken breast, fresh pasta of the day and chicken, mushroom and bacon pie. There is also a choice of sweets and a traditional Sunday roast. Brew XI is available on keg, plus Guinness, Caffreys and Carling Black Label. Dogs are permitted, but not in the dining areas. Children are welcome.
Telephone: 01827 383691.

How to get there: From the A513 between Tamworth and Alrewas, follow signs for Harlaston, to the east. The inn will be found in the centre, near the church. You can also reach the village from the A453 Tamworth to Ashby-de-la-Zouch road. Turn off at the sign for Clifton Campville and then go on to Harlaston. The inn is on the right.

Parking: There is a car park opposite the inn and also room to park elsewhere in the village.

Length of the walk: 2¼ miles. Map: OS Landranger 128 Derby and Burton-upon-Trent area (GR 216111).

About ½ mile from the start of this walk you will encounter the Mease, snaking its way through the level countryside of east Staffordshire. Beyond the river you reach the village of Edingale, before recrossing the Mease. Fishermen can often be seen beside the water on this very pleasant route.

The Walk
From the door of the pub bear left for several yards to the junction. Turn left and head down the road, between houses and bungalows. Pass the pumping station on the left and continue along the road. At this stage there are delightful views over a gentle rural landscape, divided by hedgerows and dotted with trees.

Pass a solitary cottage on the left. As the road curves right, bear left at the entrance to a white house. This is a bridleway. Follow the drive for a few yards, then swing right at a yellow waymarker. Pass to the right of an old mill and then follow the

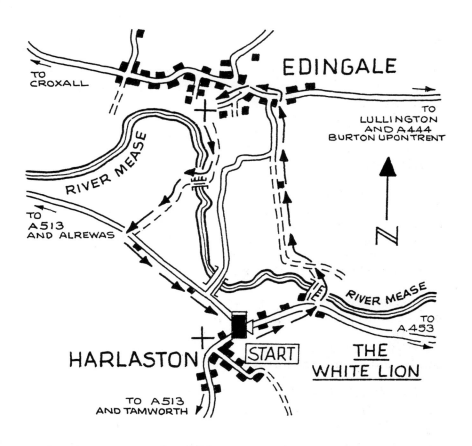

path to a concrete footbridge across the river Mease. On the right, in the distance, is the spire of Clifton Campville church, peeping between the trees. Beyond the footbridge follow a clear path across the meadow towards a line of trees and bushes.

Make for a gate and then follow the path through the trees. Ascend a bank to reach a track and turn left. Follow the track between hedgerows and soon it bends quite sharply to the right. At this point, ½ mile ahead of you, the houses of Harlaston are visible. Thick woodland interspersed with glimpses of an occasional house or cottage create a striking rural picture.

Keep to the clear, straight track and follow it past a bungalow called The Crabtrees. At the road turn right and pass the village sign for Edingale. Head for the junction and turn left towards

Croxall. When you draw level with a pub, the Black Horse, bear left into Church Lane. Follow the road between houses and cottages. Soon you come to a row of houses on the right and the entrance to Church Farm on the left. Continue down to Holy Trinity church, built in the late 19th century to replace an earlier church struck by lightning and destroyed by fire.

Just before the next road turn left into the churchyard and follow the waymarked path to the right of the church. Pass lines of gravestones and go down to a stile in the boundary. Follow a rather muddy path between fences and fields, with good views over farmland. Cross a concrete footbridge and a stile. Head across the field to the next stile and in the following field make for a clump of trees ahead. Looking back, there is a good view of the church and houses at Edingale.

Just before the trees, which are oak and beech, swing right to cross a footbridge and stile. Follow the bank of the Mease until you come to a wooden footbridge over the swirling waters of the river. Streaming water plants can easily be seen just beneath the surface.

Turn left and follow the field edge. Pass under some power cables and keep the boundary on your left all the way to the road. As you approach it, look for a wooden waymarker post. Bear left and follow the quiet lane back to Harlaston. Pass a turning on the left to Edingale. Soon you reach the inn where the walk began.